EVANGELISM MADE SLIGHTLY LESS DIFFICULT

How to Interest People Who Aren't Interested

Nick Pollard

InterVarsity Press
Downers Grove, Illinois

InterVarsity Press
P.O. Box 1400, Downers Grove, IL 60515
World Wide Web: www.ivpress.com
E-mail: mail@ivpress.com

InterVarsity Press® is the book-publishing division of InterVarsity Christian Fellowship/USA®, a student movement active on campus at hundreds of universities, colleges and schools of nursing in the United States of America, and a member movement of the International Fellowship of Evangelical Students. For information about local and regional activities, write Public Relations Dept., InterVarsity Christian Fellowship/USA, 6400 Schroeder Rd., P.O. Box 7895, Madison, WI 53707-7895.

ISBN 0-8308-1908-8

Printed in the United States of America ♻

Library of Congress Cataloging-in-Publication Data

Pollard, Nick.
    Evangelism made slightly less difficult: how to interest people who
aren't interested/Nick Pollard
        p.   cm.
    Includes bibliographical references.
    ISBN 0-8308-1908-8 (alk. paper)
    1. Evangelistic work.   2. Witness bearing (Christianity)
I. Title.
BV3790.P59   1998
269'.2—dc21   97-45682
                                                                   CIP

19	18	17	16	15	14	13	12	11	10	9	8	7	6	5	4	3	2	1
13	12	11	10	09	08	07	06	05	04	03	02	01	00	99	98	97		

For Luke, who says,
"Daddy, I'm really glad you go and tell people about Jesus,
but I really miss you when you are not here."

And for Lizzie,
who reminds me when I come home that
"Daddies are for kissing and cuddling."

93468

Foreword

"If religion is the opium of the people, Christianity is the sleeping pill!" claimed a critic of the church recently. One of the biggest mistakes the church has made is to create and then consistently reinforce the popular idea that Christianity is boring.

But after twenty-five years of being a Christian I remain fundamentally convinced that the message of the Bible is more dynamic, life-changing and relevant than anything else I've ever heard or read. Why then are we Christians putting such a large segment of the population to sleep with it?

You may not have heard of Nick Pollard. There's a very good reason for that. He doesn't frequent many Christian conferences. His time is consumed by his work with young adults in schools and universities as he passionately conveys his excitement at Jesus' message. This book reflects its author—it's just as lively, contemporary, compassionate, unpretentious and honest as Nick is himself. And it's definitely not boring!

In the pages that follow, Nick sets himself the task of explaining how to go about relating to and gaining the attention of the largest group of nonbelievers in our society today—those who simply find Christianity irrelevant. He then goes on to provide help for others who, though they are nearer to faith, still have huge questions which, unless heard and clearly answered, act as giant barriers to faith.

Nick has a unique approach to evangelism. He works by unpacking and exploring people's belief systems with them—even when they don't yet know they have them! Generally, evangelists are better talkers than listeners. Nick listens hard before he speaks. His is not the kind of inflexible evangelistic agenda which tragically has so often dominated the church and alienated its hearers. Instead he has the gift of being able to help people think through the implications of what they believe. He takes them on a journey of personal discovery as he carefully builds understanding and trust and introduces them to Jesus.

I'm convinced that a truly effective Christian communicator is one who has a deep understanding of biblical principles, a clear grasp of contemporary culture and the ability to analyze both and apply the one to the other. It's that rare combination of skills that makes Nick Pollard so well worth reading.

Steve Chalke
The Oasis Trust, London

Preface

I could never thank all those who have helped, supported and worked with me over the years. But I shall mention a few of them.

Most of all I thank my wife, Carol. Before we had children, we worked together in many missions. Though she now stays at home, she is just as vital to the ministry. I don't know how other men survive, since they are not married to her.

Thanks to the team of friends who have worked with me over the years, both on the field and in the office: Kriss Akabusi, Julia Bradley, Sue Bryan, Eden Burning, Charlotte (Charlie) Cranston, John Curle, Valmai Francis, Brian Greenaway, Matt Jones, Tricia Kenyon, Jess Loseby, John Markin, Jill Purkiss, Gavin Silver, Brussel Spaceship (as was), Steve Temple and Jayne Wells.

Thanks to my trustees, who have sought to discern God's guidance and direction for my ministry: Mary Godfree, Eric Gower, Arthur Laxton, Brian Mitchener, John Symons and John Waldron.

Thanks to my supporters, who use my daily prayer diary to pray for me, and those who support my ministry financially; we could not do it without them.

Thanks to my friends in the planning group for the Damaris Project, who have encouraged me to train other Christians as well as just getting on with evangelism myself: Alison Farnell, Eric Gower (again), Andy Hickford, Ann Holt, Phil Wall and Emlyn Williams.

Thanks to everyone at IVP-UK, especially Colin Duriez, for taking the risk of trying out this brand-new author.

Finally, special thanks to David Cook, Fellow of Green College,

Oxford, and Director of the Whitefield Institute. He took this ex-scholar, who had become woolly through years away from academia, and forced me to think clearly again. Any quality in this book is largely thanks to David; any faults are entirely my own.

Nick Pollard

Introduction

I am writing this introduction at a university in York, England, where I am currently in the middle of a campus mission. Through the window I can see groups of students walking into the student union, where I shall soon be speaking and answering questions. I am nervous, very nervous.

A good friend said to me recently, "There is one thing you'll never suffer from as an evangelist."

"What's that?" I asked.

"Constipation," he replied.

Too right! Nerves will always see to that. I didn't need prunes on my bran flakes this morning.

Why is it that evangelism is so difficult? Why is it so nerve-wracking? There are lots of reasons, and I shall seek to deal with as many as I can in this book. But don't expect that reading it will make evangelism easy; nothing can do that. All I can say is that it should help you to find evangelism slightly less difficult.

Where Do We Start?

Whenever I meet people who are not Christians and seek to help them, I usually find that they fall into one of four categories.

First, there are those who are just about ready to become Christians. Perhaps they have been thinking about Jesus for some time; they know that the Christian gospel is true, and they simply need someone to call them to respond. I have no illusions about what I am doing for those people; I am just picking ripe fruit. In fact, sometimes the fruit is so ripe on the tree that all it takes is an old cow to bump into the trunk for it to fall off.[1] That's what I sometimes feel like: an old cow going around bumping into trees.

Second, there are some who really want to become Christians but are holding back because they have lots of questions and doubts which they need to deal with first. One student said to me, "I think I want to become a Christian, but before I do I need to know that it is actually true." He was full of questions and was looking for satisfactory answers.

Third, there are those who are genuinely interested but are not really sure where to begin because they know so little about Jesus. Often they haven't got questions because, at the minute, they don't really know what the issues are. Over the years, some people have said to me, "Thank you ever so much for coming. I don't know anything about Jesus because I've never been to church or read the Bible, but I do want to find out."

So far there doesn't seem to be much of a problem, does there? If everyone fell into one of these three categories, evangelism would be pretty straightforward. As long as we are able to teach them about Jesus, answer their questions and then lead them to Christ, we are home free. We could do all our friends in a few days—and next week start on India.

Although these are three clearly identifiable categories into which some people fit, the fact is that they account for only a minority of the total. The vast majority of people today are in a fourth category: they are simply not interested. Some are openly hostile, but others just seem apathetic about the whole subject. They are quite happy with their own non-Christian worldviews, thank you very much: "If you want to believe all this stuff about Jesus, that's OK for you, but leave me alone."

If we are going to be effective in evangelism, we must be able to help people in each of these four categories. That is why the book is divided into four. Each part will consider one of the categories, and I shall take them in reverse order because that is the logical sequence through which we would expect people to pass. (In fact, it is rarely as simple as that; most people seem to bounce around between categories or mixtures of them.)

In part one, we shall consider how to help people who are not at all interested in the gospel because they are quite happy with what they currently believe. This is the longest part of the book, not just because it deals with the largest category, but also because we Christians are just waking up to the fact that this group exists at all—so here is where many of us need a lot of help. I will introduce you to the term *positive deconstruction* (sorry it's a bit long, but I couldn't think of a shorter one). This is the term I use to describe the process of helping people who are currently comfortable with their non-Christian beliefs to think again about them—and possibly to become uncomfortable with them, so much so that they begin to want to find out about Jesus.

In part two, we will look at "gospel proclamation" and consider how we might understand the gospel so clearly that we can communicate it simply, in a language that people can understand.

In part three, we will look at what is called "apologetics." That has nothing to do with apologizing. It is the task of answering people's questions about our faith—giving the reason for the hope we have. I shall consider some general principles for answering people's questions and then explore just a few of the major issues which seem to crop up time and time again.

In part four, we will consider how we can lead individuals to faith in Christ. If we can help them through all the other stages but don't know how to help them move into a personal relationship with Jesus, we really are going to let them down. I was a Christian for many years before I had any idea how to help someone take that initial step of faith. Perhaps it's a good thing nobody asked me.

As an evangelist I work mainly in universities and colleges, so I spend most of my time trying to help students and young people. This book is therefore written from that perspective. But I hope the content will be just as relevant to you, whoever you are trying to help. You may find you have to apply the ideas at a different level, use different words and go at a different speed. But you should find that the principle is just the same.

Now, before we move into the book, I want to set the four parts in their proper context by looking at a passage of the Bible that gives us some vital teaching about evangelism.

1

It Doesn't Have to Be Quite So Hard

GOD DOESN'T JUST CALL US *to get on with evangelism without* also giving us clear instructions about how we are to do it. Perhaps the most straightforward teaching about evangelism is given in a passage from Paul's letter to the church at Colosse. Let's look at it, section by section.

> Devote yourselves to prayer, being watchful and thankful. And pray for us, too, that God may open a door for our message, so that we may proclaim the mystery of Christ, for which I am in chains. Pray that I may proclaim it clearly, as I should. Be wise in the way you act toward outsiders; make the most of every opportunity. Let your conversation be always full of grace, seasoned with salt, so that you may know how to answer every-one. (Col 4:2-6)

This instruction falls naturally into two parts. The first three verses are all about prayer: "devote yourselves to prayer," "pray for us" and so on. The last two verses are all about evangelism, with phrases like "Be wise in the way you act toward outsiders" and "Let your conversation be always. . . ." These two activities must always go together. Prayer is talking to God about people, and evangelism is talking to people about God. We cannot do one without the other.

Now if the two go together, you can start with whichever you find easier. If you find prayer easier, start by praying for specific people—and you will find that God begins to give you opportunities to talk to them about him. If, on the other hand, you find evangelism easier, start by talking to people about Jesus—and you will find that you are soon driven to prayer. If you find both difficult, you really are in need of this book, so read on.

Let's look at prayer and evangelism separately.

Prayer

Three prayers are described in the passage above.

First, Paul says, "Pray for us . . . that God may open a door for our message." Paul calls us to imitate him, so let's apply this to ourselves. We are to pray for opportunities to talk to people about Jesus. I wonder whether or not you would like to pray that prayer. Would you pray that tomorrow you'll get an opportunity to talk to the person who sits next to you, or to someone on the bus?

I wonder how you feel about that. People often look a bit uncertain when I suggest praying like this. They are not really keen on praying this prayer, for the simple reason that they're scared that God will answer it! Are you like that? Are you terrified that somehow there will be an opportunity to talk to someone about Jesus and you won't know what to do? Are you afraid you'll get embarrassed, let the opportunity pass by and then feel guilty about it for days? You might well be. And let me tell you a secret: I'm scared too! In the past I have wimped out of so many God-given opportunities that it's understandable I'm not eager to get more chances to fail. But, thankfully, God knows that we are all scared about this.

That's why we're told to pray the second prayer: "so that we may proclaim the mystery of Christ." We are told to pray that we'll take up the opportunity and proclaim the gospel of Jesus. How about praying that prayer too? Pray that God will give you an opportunity and that you will take it up. Does that make it better? Well, if you're anything like me, it does help a bit, because if God answers both prayers, I know I won't just stand there looking stupid.

But I'm still scared. What worries me is that I'll get an opportunity to talk to someone about Jesus and take it, but then just make a mess of it. Does that worry you in the same way? Perhaps, like me, you have talked to people about Jesus only to feel afterward that you have made a real mess of it. Do you find yourself wringing your hands and saying, "If only I'd thought of . . ." or "Why on earth didn't I say . . . ?" Again, we can thank God that he knows our weaknesses.

That's why he gives us the third prayer: "Pray that I may proclaim it clearly, as I should." We are told to pray that we won't botch it up. (That's a loose translation, but basically it's what Paul is saying.)

Do you see how important it is to take those three prayers together? We must pray that God will give us opportunities to talk to people about Jesus, that we'll take those opportunities, and that, when we do, we'll be able to proclaim the gospel clearly, as we should. Perhaps you might like to put the book down for a minute and pray as this passage of the Bible asks you to, voicing those three prayers.

In the rest of this book I am not going to talk much more about prayer. That isn't because I don't think it's important—of course I do. But there are many excellent books on prayer, and I want to concentrate on the subject of evangelism. So let's move on to that now.

Evangelism

Verses 5 and 6 give a series of instructions about how we should engage in evangelism. Let's look at those in order.

First, we are told to "be wise in the way you act toward outsiders." God calls us to be wise, to use our brains. Some people seem to think that God made a great mistake when he created our brains, that he deeply repented of it the next day, and that ever since then he's been trying to stop us from using them! But that isn't the truth.

Of course, our brains have become corrupted by sin, but we need to pray that God will renew our minds (see Rom 12:2). Peter Cotterell, former principal of London Bible College, says that, when he became a Christian, "for the first time in my life I could think straight." If you find you can't think straight, perhaps you need to cry out to God, asking him to continue his work in you and to give you "spiritual wisdom and understanding" (Col 1:9). God created our brains, and he wants us to use them in his service.

When I first started in evangelism, I found that just ten minutes talking with a non-Christian about Jesus meant that I then had to spend ten hours studying, thinking and picking the brains of older, wiser Christians. Evangelism is not easy, particularly in today's culture, and if we are serious about reaching people with the gospel we must be serious about wrestling with difficult, complex issues.

I'm sorry that some of the issues we shall look at in this book are quite complicated, but I'm afraid there is nothing I can do about it. I want to be a simple evangelist proclaiming a simple gospel message, but, unfortunately, I have to face the fact that the people I am trying to help live in a complex world. If you find some parts of this book difficult, please don't give up; just skip the hard bits and learn from the easier ones. Later, perhaps, you might have another go at it and find the hard bits not quite so hard after all.

I have some friends who have Ph.D.'s in theoretical physics and others whose only "B.Sc." is a Bronze Swimming certificate. But the truth is that God can and does use each of them in evangelism, if they are willing to give themselves totally to him. No matter what level of education you have reached, you do have a brain, and God calls you to use it and develop it as much as you are able.

Next, we are told to "make the most of every opportunity." It is important to note that we are not told to "make the opportunity." When I first understood this, it came as a great relief to me. I had always felt under a tremendous pressure that I had, somehow, to manufacture opportunities to talk to people about Jesus.

How to Lose Friends and Irritate People

Have you ever been on a bus journey or at a meal with friends and found yourself desperately trying to think of ways of manipulating the conversation around to Jesus? I used to feel that pressure, particularly when there was a major evangelistic campaign and I wanted to have some kind of story to tell in the testimony slot on Sunday. I guess that when I did that, I was motivated more by a desire not to feel like a failure than by a real concern to help people.

If we give in to this pressure, it tends to lead to some very strange conversations. What do you do if all the other person wants to talk about with you is the excellent taramasalata they had at lunch? How do you work that around to Jesus? That's a bit of a challenge.

You might have a brainwave and say: "Taramasalata—that's Greek food, isn't it? You know, a guy called Paul traveled around Greece talking to people about Jesus. Now, as we're on the subject of Jesus, can I explain the gospel to you?" That's a great way to lose friends and irritate people.

This passage is clear: We are not told to make the opportunity, just to make the most of the opportunity as it arises. That's very liberating. It sets us free to have real, relaxed conversations with other people and to trust God to provide the opportunities—which he will do, if we are praying the three prayers that Paul gives us in these verses.

Some friends of mine eat regularly in their local pub. They are very friendly, chatty people, who easily get into conversations with the other regulars. From the start they made a decision that they would never initiate a conversation about Jesus or try to manipulate one around to him. Yet almost every time they are in the pub someone starts talking to *them* about Jesus.

Of course, "making the most of opportunities" doesn't mean going on and on and on. I used to feel under pressure not just to make opportunities but also to make results. Somehow I felt that I had failed if the person I manipulated into a conversation wasn't converted in ten minutes and baptized on Sunday. This is another pressure from which we need to be released.

I don't know about you, but I naturally seemed to assume that, once I had a chance to talk to someone about Jesus, this was the only opportunity I would ever get with this person. So I used to think, *This is it—at last I have my one opportunity! I must give it all I've got.* So what did I do? I turbo-charged my tongue and talked and talked and talked.

I cringe when I look back at times when I must have been the biggest bore in the world. And do you know what happened to the people I talked to? No, nor do I—because I didn't see many of them again. They must have gone away thinking, *That's the last time I'm ever going to talk to any Christian.* I certainly put them off.

When I realized that making the most of the opportunity means helping people in the best way possible, I began to see that I should leave them thinking, *That was interesting. I want to find out more. I must talk to him about this again.* Nowadays, when I have an opportunity to talk to people, I try to leave them hungry to read the Bible, to come to a particular meeting, to talk to someone else—anything to find out more about Jesus.

That's why I believe that starting to talk to people about Jesus is only the second hardest thing to do in evangelism. It is difficult to take up opportunities and to begin talking to people about him. But that isn't the hardest thing to do, it's only the second hardest. The hardest is to stop talking once we've started.

In practical terms this means trying to give regular opportunities for people (if they wish) to stop the conversation or move it on to something else without feeling embarrassed. Sometimes, of course, that doesn't happen, and I talk with people for a long time. But in that case at least I am sure that they are talking because they want to, not because I am pushing them into it.

Give People Room

Some years ago I was doing some street evangelism with my home church. One morning I spent about an hour and a half talking with one man. You might think I must have been babbling on and on. But I wasn't. I knew that he wanted to talk and didn't want to stop. What happened throughout most of the conversation was that he would ask me a question, and I would answer it, take a step back and say,

"OK?" This made it very easy for him to say "Thank you" and carry on to do his shopping. But he didn't. He would take one step forward and say, "What about this, then . . . ?"

I would answer his question and again take a step back. He would take a step forward and ask another. After an hour and a half of this little dance we were down to the other end of the street. But at least we knew that he was in control. He could stop the conversation easily any time he wanted.

Of course, there is a way of giving people opportunities to end the conversation and yet providing a small "hook" that intrigues them and encourages them to keep on thinking about Jesus. There is a story told of Billy Graham at a dinner party. Someone asked him, "Billy, have you always enjoyed going to church?" He could have used that as a cue for a sermon, but he didn't. Rather, he replied, "No, I used to hate going to church, until I was eighteen and something happened that completely changed my mind."

Now what do you think the next question was? "What happened when you were eighteen?"

Well, it probably was that, but it could just as easily have been, "That's very interesting. Could you pass the salt, please?" You see, he offered them an easy opportunity to change the subject if they wished, but in his reply he also provided a little hook.

We are to make the most of every opportunity, but in most cases that will mean leaving people hungry for more.

Now let's return to Paul's text, and we will see that verse 6 gives us three clear instructions.

First, it says: "let your conversation be always full of grace." We have a gospel of grace and love and reconciliation. And we must communicate it in a way that demonstrates this. Evangelism isn't just about saying certain things. It's about being a certain person and living in a certain way. The heart of the gospel is love, and love must be in the center of our hearts as we seek to communicate this gospel to others.

Our motive must never be to win a battle or prove ourselves right, but rather to live out a life of genuine, sacrificial love. We are called to display the kind of love that kept Jesus on the cross when he could have wiggled his little finger and wiped everyone out with a thunderbolt. Because of love, he hung there and took all that was thrown at him.

As you read this book, you will soon realize that I can tell as many stories about my failures as an evangelist as I can about my successes. For instance, I became a Christian when I was fifteen and living in the town of Bath. The moment I came to Christ I was so excited about my new relationship with him I wanted everyone to hear about it. So I decided to go down to the city center and give out tracts. Full of enthusiasm and zeal, I thought I was going to see the whole of Bath converted that morning.

Most people took pity on me and accepted the leaflets I offered. But one man was laden down with shopping; he obviously wanted to get to his car, and he didn't want to stop. I wasn't thinking about him, though; I was on a mission. I approached him and said, "I want to give you this tract."

"No thanks," he replied, and walked past.

I wasn't going to be put off by that, so I ran after him and said, a little more loudly, "I want to give you this tract."

This obviously annoyed him. He looked at me angrily and said, in an even louder voice, "No thanks!"

Well, that made me angry too, so I said, more loudly still, *"I want to give you this tract."*

At that he stopped and shouted at me, *"What the ——— do you want to give it to me for?"*

By now I was livid. I could have decked him. I shouted out, " *'cause God loves you!"*

Clearly, I had told the man that God loved him. But I really don't think I communicated that message.

If we tell people of God's love without at the same time demonstrating that love, our words are empty and hypocritical. God has given us a gospel of love and reconciliation. We must communicate it in that way. The message of Jesus tells us that God wants us to live in a love relationship with him and a love relationship with other people. So our evangelism must center around the offer and provision of loving relationships.

Sometimes, during a mission, Christian students tell me they have just had "a big argument with my friends about God." I often reply, "Oh dear, I'm so sorry."

Now, that isn't the reply they expected to receive. So they sometimes continue, "Don't worry, I won the argument."

"Yes," I say, "but did you lose the person?"

We are called by God to serve people, not to argue with them. God is on their side, and so must we be also.

Speaking the Truth with Love

I shall always remember a student telling me how he had become a Christian in one of my missions. He said that it was the open debates which had made the difference for him. But it turned out that it wasn't any clever answers to the difficult questions that helped him especially. Rather, he said that it was the loving and gracious way in which I had treated the aggressive questioners who were trying to have a go at me. He added that he too wanted to have that kind of love for people, and so he cried out to Jesus to change him.

That doesn't mean that we must become slushy, sentimental, pink marshmallows. Genuine love has teeth when necessary. That's why verse 6 also says that our conversation, as well as being full of grace, must be "seasoned with salt." Salt added to a meal brings out the flavor, while salt put on a wound stings but acts as an antiseptic. Our conversations need to be the same. We must be gracious, but we must also demonstrate the true love that warns people of personal danger.

Imagine that I see a shady-looking character tampering with the brakes of your car. I can tell that if you drive off in it, you are likely to be killed. What is the most loving thing for me to do? I might think, *I mustn't say anything because I don't want to worry them. I don't want them to be upset. It would be far better for them to drive off happy.* Or is the loving response to warn you of the danger you are in? Certainly, my warning must be gracious (if I am antagonistic and aggressive you are not likely listen to me), but it must also be seasoned with salt. It must cut into the situation in some way by communicating the truth.

Let me give you an example. Some years ago I was working with the Billy Graham Association, setting up a big mission. A certain printer did a lot of work for us. He made no effort to disguise the fact that he wasn't a Christian, but he was happy to have the business. One day I called at his office to collect the printing and was surprised by the first words he said to me.

"I've been reading your publicity," he said. "I suppose it's good that people are interested in finding out about God, isn't it?"

I could have taken that as an opportunity to preach at him. But that wouldn't have been gracious, and it would probably have put him off for a long time. A gracious response, seasoned with salt, might have been to say, "Yes, it is. What about you? Are you interested in finding out about God?"

This question isn't pushy or unloving, but there is a sense in which it graciously cuts into the real situation and brings it down to him personally. I wish I had said it. That would have been good. But I didn't. All I did was smile and say, "Yes. Is the printing ready?"

So remember, when you make an attempt at evangelism and totally blow it, you are in good company! Well, mine, anyway.

Finally, the passage says that we must "know how to answer everyone." Notice that it doesn't say that we are to know how to preach thirty-minute sermons to people. For most of us, our evangelism takes place in the form of conversations over coffee or at the bus stop. In these situations no one has ever said to me, "You are a Christian. Please preach to me for half an hour." Often they are happy to engage in discussion and debate with me, but they don't want to hear a sermon.

There can be a problem, then, for those of us whose only regular model of evangelism is the pastor "preaching the gospel" on Sunday. That's why many Christians think they are useless at evangelism. "People don't listen to me like they do to the pastor." Of course they don't! The evangelistic sermon is a very unusual form of evangelism. In most everyday situations, you can't even get a sentence out without being interrupted with a torrent of questions and objections. If we are to be equipped to help people in the more normal situations we face day by day in the real world, we must be able to answer their genuine questions.

Of course, different people have different questions. It is my prayer that the four sections of this book will be of help to you as you seek to serve people whatever questions they ask. Some will be a brush-off: "Why should I be interested in Jesus? I'm happy as I am." We'll think about questions like that in part one.

Other questions will stem from a person's interest in finding out about Christian faith: "What is it you actually believe as a Christian?" "Why do you live the way you do?" We'll look at questions like those in part two.

Still other people will be full of questions that express doubts about the truth of Christian belief: "How can God be loving if he allows suffering?" "Hasn't science disproved Christianity?" We'll consider some of these questions in part three.

Finally, some will ask, "What must I do to be saved?" In about a quarter of the open debates I do with students, someone asks me a question like this. We'll look at it in part four.

Part One

Helping People Who Don't Seem Interested

2

What Has
Gone Wrong?

MANY PEOPLE SEEM TO ASSUME *that hearing about Jesus is* only marginally more exciting than tidying their sock drawer. So they are not interested. I find this to be the case with most students. Others find the same with colleagues in the office or neighbors over the backyard fence. How can we help people like this?

Obviously we must spend time with them, to build meaningful relationships with them. We need to demonstrate the love and power of Jesus in our lives as well as in our words. But we also have to be able to help them think again about the ideas and beliefs they have picked up.

In this part of the book, I want to help you develop your ability to reach the ever-increasing number of people who are simply not interested in hearing about Jesus because they are quite happy with their own views, thank you very much. If people are currently comfortable with their non-Christian worldview, we need to know how to help them become uncomfortable with it, so that they may become interested in looking at Jesus. But before we can consider this solution, we must think in more depth about the nature of the problem.

Things Ain't What They Used to Be

One Sunday morning in 1742, John Wesley stood in a Newcastle street and sang from Psalm 100. A large crowd gathered to listen, and he told them, "At five p.m., with God's help, I design to preach here again." That afternoon thousands of people turned out to hear him.

Suppose I were to do the same thing in Newcastle today. Imagine I sang a psalm in the middle of Main Street. Would hundreds gather to listen? Would thousands come back to hear me preach? No way. They'd be out of there so fast I wouldn't see them for the clouds of dust! There is no doubt that things have changed. We now live in a very different culture, and nowhere is this more evident than among the emerging generation.

Of course, most of our youth workers recognize shifts in youth culture and try to respond appropriately. Thankfully, there is much to help us. Countless books and magazine articles tell us how we can conduct our evangelism in a more relevant way. Many point to cultural features such as clothes and music.

Clothes are important. If I walked onto a college campus looking like a complete nerd, students would not want to be seen with me. I would simply reinforce the common idea that to be a Christian you've got to have all the intelligence of a marshmallow and all the personality of a dead goldfish.

Similarly, music is important. Today's generation will be attracted by good musicians playing culturally relevant music, but you won't draw much of a crowd with Moody and Sankey hymns.

As important as these and other aspects of youth culture may be, however, they are all largely peripheral. If we do no more than adopt their clothes, music and style, we are simply engaging in a sham, a hollow advertising trick. In order to reach this generation, we need to respond at a far deeper level. That is, we must address the changes taking place in their underlying worldviews.

Steve Chalke has said, "Most youth workers are very good at understanding contemporary youth culture in terms of clothes, music, language and behavior. All of these are important, but, if the church is to deal with causes rather than just symptoms, we need specialist help in identifying and responding to the underlying worldviews which so many young people are absorbing unconsciously."

In this chapter I will look at the challenge we face as we try to reach those growing up among a wide range of attractive worldviews. We shall see how these views are being adopted by today's generation and how this affects their thinking in general and their attitude to Jesus in particular. It will become clear that, if we are to reach people today, we need to develop the ability to help people to discover the inadequacies of the worldviews they have adopted.

But first we must understand what we mean by a worldview.

Two Definitions of *Worldview*

The term *worldview* has recently become a buzzword among many Christians. But do we really understand what it means? In fact, the term appears to be used in two rather different ways, which could be characterized as "bottom up" and "top down."

1. The bottom-up worldview model. Some people use the term *worldview* to describe the conclusion that a person comes to after looking at the world and asking the most fundamental questions about it: "Who am I?" "Where am I?" "What's wrong with the world?" and "What's the remedy?" Everyone asks these questions at some time and in some way, although we may not be aware of the fact that we are doing so. According to this use of the term, people take the answers they find for these fundamental questions and combine them to form their worldview.

For instance, they may answer these questions in the following way: "I am a child of God. I am living in the world which God created to be enjoyed by me and others. The world is in a mess because we have turned our backs on God, and we need to return to God, through Christ, in repentance and faith." When put together like this, these answers lead to a Christian worldview.

Or they may give a very different answer, such as the following: "I am a collection of atoms and molecules that work together to give the impression that I am an individual soul. I live in a vast universe which came about by chance and is ultimately purposeless, and in one sense there is nothing wrong with the world since it simply is how it is. Because I have evolved to a higher level, however, I can now decide that the world is not how I want it to be. Science will enable me to have mastery over our world and to change it to suit me." When combined like this, these answers lead to a scientific materialist worldview. Either way, the worldview is considered to be what is derived from the answers given to the fundamental questions about life. We start by asking the fundamental questions and end with a particular view of the world.

2. The top-down worldview model. Others seem to use the term *worldview* in a different way. They see it not as the conclusion at which people arrive but as the point from which they start. It is the way people view the world, the spectacles through which they look, the grid upon which they organize reality.

According to this definition, a worldview is not a "view of the world" derived from particular answers to the fundamental questions, but rather a "way of viewing the world" which brings about those particular answers. Thus, according to this use of the term, people will give particular answers to the fundamental questions because they hold a certain worldview, rather than holding that worldview because they have given particular answers to the fundamental questions.

For instance, the answers people give to the question "Who am I?" will depend upon the worldview they hold. If it is a Christian worldview, they will say, "I am a child of God." If it is a scientific materialist worldview they will say, "I am a collection of atoms and molecules which work together to give the impression that I am an individual soul." Either way, the answers to the fundamental questions are derived from the worldview. That is, they start with a particular "way of viewing the world" and consequently end with a certain set of answers to the fundamental questions about life.

A More Complete Model?

Both the bottom-up and top-down definitions provide valuable insights into what happens when people develop and maintain their worldviews. But each gives only a part of the picture. A better model, which would give us a more complete understanding, would come from a combination of both.

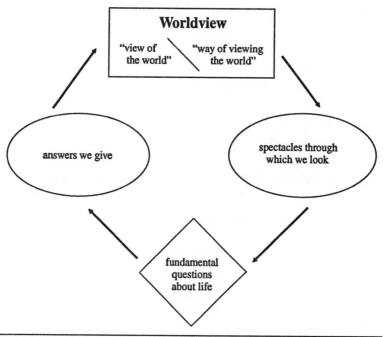

Figure 1. A Circular Worldview Model

As individuals develop, they do seem to adopt certain answers to the fundamental questions of life. These answers are put together into a comprehensive system—a view of the world. At the same time, however, this view of the world becomes the way they view the world. It becomes the spectacles through which they look, the grid upon which they organize reality. This view affects the way they answer the fundamental questions of life, and so on. (See figure 1.)

If we understand worldviews this way, we can see why they are so hard to change. They tend to become firmly entrenched because they constantly reinforce themselves through their self-sustaining feedback loop.[1]

Let me illustrate how this works in practice. Some years ago I sat in a college coffee bar discussing ancient mythology with an avowed atheist. We both remarked upon the wide occurrence of myths that speak of gods becoming human in order to save the world. But we each looked at this very differently.

The atheist looked through his worldview spectacles and explained these myths as examples of stories written out of our psychological need for a savior-god. Thus, giving these answers, he reinforced his belief that all religion is purely psychological wish-fulfillment.

On the other hand, I looked through my Christian worldview spectacles and explained these myths as examples of how God had written his plan of salvation on our hearts so that even those who have not yet heard the gospel somehow know it deep down. I thus reinforced my belief in how much God loves us and wants us to come back to him. In this way, two mutually contradictory worldviews were both reinforced by exactly the same piece of evidence. We decided that we both needed to be prepared to step back and think again.

If we are going to help people change their worldviews, then, we must try to help them step outside their feedback loop (inasmuch as that is possible), to ask some difficult questions and to explore alternative interpretations. And we need to be prepared to do the same ourselves.

This presents a challenge to those of us who are attempting to reach people with the gospel of Jesus, particularly in this culture which is both postmodern and post-Christian. Let's look at this challenge now.

Worldviews in Our Postmodern and Post-Christian Culture

We live at an unusual time. Today's generation is emerging into a culture that is postmodern and post-Christian. It is a world that offers them no one answer, or even the prospect of finding one, but rather a wide range of attractive worldviews from which they can mix and match in any way that suits them.

A postmodern culture. Modern culture is fast turning into postmodern culture. This change has major implications for the way we conduct our evangelism, and we will return to it in chapters six and ten. For now, however, let me give a very brief introduction to the changes taking place.

Two centuries ago the Enlightenment (or Age of Reason) brought about a big change in people's thinking. Essentially, philosophers rejected the dogma of the church and placed their hope in human ability to reason. This ushered in a time of great optimism. People thought we would be able to solve all our problems. The world was going to get better and better. We could find the answers to life ourselves. As Dr Edmund Leach put it, "Men have become like gods. . . . Science offers us total mastery over our environment and destiny." The culture that was based upon the Enlightenment, and in which we have lived since, is called *modernism.*

In recent years, however, people have begun to realize that the hopes, dreams and promises of the Enlightenment have not been fulfilled. There is even a growing anti-science movement as people reflect upon the nuclear and environmental threat, the fears of biogenetic engineering and the failure of orthodox medicine to deliver what people think it promised.

Many philosophers believe that modernism is coming to an end. As Lesslie Newbigin has pointed out, "Cultures are born and die. The question now is whether we are at a point where a culture is approaching death." Many argue that we are moving into a new cultural period, which is being called *postmodernism.* This new culture cannot even be named except in relation to what preceded it. No one can say what it is; all we can say is what it is not. It is not modern; it is postmodern.

One of the major pessimistic assumptions of postmodernism is that there is no one universal answer. To use a buzzword of the postmoderns, there are no metanarratives. This, of course, has a major effect upon a generation that might otherwise be seeking answers. Many postmoderns will say, "We are not seekers after truth. What's the point, if there is no truth to find?"

While this change has taken place, another, not unrelated, shift has also been occurring.

A post-Christian culture. There was a time when Western culture could be called Christian. That doesn't mean that everyone living in it was a Christian, but there was essentially just one worldview offered—a Christian one.

I was a teenager twenty years ago. My generation received a clear Christian heritage. We knew much of the Bible. The parents of many of us went to church, and many of us did as well. We were taught Christian religious education at school, and the prevailing ethic was Judeo-Christian.

This is no longer the case. Most of today's generation have no such heritage. Many of the students with whom I work day by day know almost nothing of the Bible and have rarely, if ever, gone to church. They are not encouraged to do so by their parents. Indeed, many of those who become Christians today face parental opposition to their newfound faith.

Most of my generation chose to reject the claims of Christ, but most of today's generation don't even know what those are. When Christians spoke to me of God, sin, heaven, hell or salvation, I generally knew what they meant. But today's generation largely do not.

Many Choices
This postmodern, post-Christian culture presents today's generation with a developing mosaic of worldviews from which they can select. There is not one worldview offered—there are many, and Christianity is just one on the list.

As Christianity has been put on the shelf, so a wide range of other worldviews have been developed in our culture, or have been imported from another culture, or a combination of both. There are too many to list, and they are growing all the time. But they range from secular humanism to Eastern mysticism, from scientific materialism to wicca paganism.

This shift is having a profound effect upon people today. The generation that has no Christian heritage does not have *no* heritage at all. If that were the case, they would be crying out for the gospel in order to have some kind of worldview upon which to base their lives. But members of today's generation do have worldviews, having adopted them from among the range of non-Christian heritages available.

Attractive worldviews. A major driving force behind the adoption of these alternative worldviews is the fact that so many of them are very attractive. They speak of personal fulfillment, self-actualization or a world without any prescriptive morality.

In our consumer-oriented society, people are looking for the most appealing range of products on offer. I have even had non-Christians sit me down and say, in all seriousness, "I've looked at a number of religions so far. Now tell me what Christianity can offer." It is as if they were selecting a new washing machine, shopping around to find the one with the best features.

Pick-and-mix worldviews. In my experience most people seem to have adopted their worldviews pragmatically (that is, they choose those which work for them). Doing it this way enables them to live how they want to. Very rarely do I come across people who live in a certain way because of what they believe. Rather, most people seem to believe something because they want to live in a certain way. They are attracted to a belief not because they see that it is true but because it justifies some behavior which they find particularly appealing.

In turn, this pragmatism necessarily leads to a pick-and-mix adoption of worldviews. As people face different situations, they wish to behave in different ways. Consequently, they have to believe different things. So, instead of adopting one complete worldview, they pick bits of different ones and mix them together.

A mixture of contradictory beliefs. In many cases the bits they have picked and mixed together are actually self-contradictory. For instance, a student may be a scientific materialist when she is working in her laboratory. At this time she sees consciousness as some kind of illusion and love as simply an evolutionary mecha-

nism that enables us to propagate the species. When she walks out
the door to go on a date with her new boyfriend, however, does she
still believe this? I don't think so.

There are those who try to be entirely consistent, but most don't.
They hold mutually contradictory elements of different worldviews.

Two Important Consequences for Today's Generation

Two important consequences result, with significant implications
for those of us who are seeking to reach today's generation with the
gospel.

First, people are reluctant to think clearly about their worldview.
Second, they are particularly reluctant to take seriously anyone who
makes absolute claims or demands—especially Jesus.

A reluctance to think clearly. Teachers and youth leaders know
all too well how hard it is to get members of today's generation to
think clearly. Why? I suggest that there are at least two major
reasons.

First, the postmodern world in which they live tells them that
there is no answer. If that is the case, why should they bother to
look for it?

Second, when they do think, they come across the contradictions
in the bits of different worldviews they have developed. This in turn
leads them to lose their confidence in thinking.

Come with me into the mind of an average young person. She is
growing up in a postmodern, post-Christian culture surrounded by
many attractive worldviews. She has picked and mixed from them
and now has a varied collection of beliefs about life, the universe
and everything. Unfortunately (and necessarily, given the way in
which they have been adopted), many of her beliefs contradict one
another. She, however, is blissfully unaware of this, since she
doesn't usually think about what she believes. She manages to keep
different parts of her life, and the beliefs that go with them, in
separate compartments.

The problem starts when she does begin to think clearly about
her worldview. Then the contradictions start to bubble to the

surface. Suddenly everything that seemed so straightforward has become muddled. What has happened? She was all right when she was just getting on with her life and taking each bit as it came. Things were easy then. But now it's so complicated. She doesn't seem to understand anything any more. This can't be right. Of course not. What caused this problem? It must be *thinking* that has done it. That's the problem. Far better not to think. Yes, that's it—don't think, just live.

And that is what many people do. Don't think—just experience life on the surface. But that is not all. There is more.

A reluctance to look at the absolute. Given that our young person already holds a set of contradictory beliefs, it is not a problem for her to adopt one more, even if it makes absolute claims or demands, provided she is not alerted to this. She is already managing to ignore one set of contradictions, so one more is not going to make much difference.

What will cause a problem, however, is making the absolute claims or demands so explicit that they cannot be ignored. If that is done, the extra idea will be resisted or, more likely, conveniently ignored.

This is the case with Jesus, if properly understood. Of course, a liberalized, watered-down Jesus could be accepted into someone's mixture of beliefs. But the real historical Jesus cannot. His radical and exclusive claims are too explicit for that.

The Need

Clearly, deep and far-reaching changes are taking place in our culture. How then can we respond to them in our evangelism? As we saw at the beginning of this chapter, it is no good trying to respond to these deep changes at a surface level. Wearing the right clothes or playing the right music will not, in itself, solve the problem. Neither can we change the content of the gospel in order to make it more attractive. This is God's message for all time, and it is not for us to chop it around or water it down. Nor would it be right just to give in to the culture and try to present the gospel in ways which don't require people to think. We are called to something far more than just life on the surface.

There is, however, something we can do. We can find ways to help today's generation think about their worldviews so that, in turn, we can then help them think about the life and teaching of Jesus. If they are currently comfortable with their hodgepodge of different worldviews, we must help them become uncomfortable with it. We must encourage them to step outside their worldview feedback loops and ask themselves the difficult questions. Perhaps then they will be interested in looking at Jesus. To this end I offer you the approach I call "positive deconstruction." What on earth is that? Read on.

3

What On Earth Is Positive Deconstruction?

MANY CHRISTIANS ASK ME about my ministry. For a long time conversations usually developed like this.

'What do you do?"

"I'm an evangelist."

"Oh! It must be great to spend all your time talking to people about Jesus."

"I wish! I wish I could spend all my time talking to people about Jesus. There is no one better to talk about, and I do as much as I can. The problem is that many of the people with whom I spend time are simply not interested. They are quite happy with their own views. They don't want to talk about Jesus, but they will talk about whatever it is they believe. So I spend a lot of time discussing Friedrich Nietzsche or Søren Kierkegaard or Kurt Cobain or Madonna or Richard Dawkins or Stephen Hawking."

"You mean you're into apologetics?"

"Well, no, this isn't apologetics. Apologetics is 'giving a reasoned defense for your faith.' I do a lot of that, of course, but much of the time I'm with people who can't see the point of questioning my faith because they're quite happy with their own—nor do they even know where to begin with questions. So I spend a lot of time questioning *them*. I ask them what they believe, why they believe it and what difference it makes to their lives. Ultimately, I'm trying to help them discover the inadequacies of the ideas they've adopted."

"So what is it you're doing?"

"A good question. I know what I am doing. And I'm not alone; others are doing it. But it doesn't seem to be called anything."

A Solution

After many conversations like this, it became clear that a new name was needed here. That is why I eventually settled on the term *positive deconstruction.*

The process is *deconstruction* because I am helping people to deconstruct (that is, take apart) what they believe in order to look carefully at the belief and analyze it. The process is *positive* because this deconstructing is done in a positive way—in order to replace the false belief with something better. There are none of the negative connotations that are sometimes associated with the branch of literary criticism known as deconstructionism, but rather a positive search for truth.

The process of positive deconstruction recognizes and affirms the elements of truth to which individuals already hold, but it also helps them discover for themselves the inadequacies of the underlying worldviews they have absorbed. The aim is to awaken a heart response that says, "I am not so sure that what I believe is right after all. I want to find out more about Jesus." At last they are taking their first steps along the road toward faith in Christ.

A Parable

When I was an undergraduate, I bought my first car. It had a good chassis and most of the body was OK. But that was about all that could be said in its favor. The engine was worn out, the gear box crunched pathetically and the suspension was broken. It just about got me around, but it wasn't really much good. Some time later I heard about another car, of the same make and model. It contained lots of new parts which were in good condition, but unfortunately it had just been written off in an accident. I immediately bought it and set about taking both cars completely apart.

This wasn't the negative deconstruction of a vandal but, rather, the positive deconstruction of a mechanic. I looked carefully at each part to see whether it was any good. If it was, I kept it. If it wasn't, I threw it away. Eventually I put all the pieces together, started it up (much to my mother's amazement) and found I now had a very good car. There wasn't actually much left of my original car. Some parts were good enough to keep. Most of them had been replaced. But I wasn't sad, I was delighted—for I had something far better.

A Warning

It seems to me that there are two big mistakes one could make with positive deconstruction.

One danger is to assume that it isn't needed. It's very simple to say, "All we need to do is pray for people," or "All we need to do is love people." It's simple—but it simply isn't true. Sometimes Christians ask me, "Why don't you just preach Jesus to students?"

I, in turn, ask them, "Have you ever visited planet Earth?"

In today's culture, where people are unconsciously absorbing elements of so many attractive non-Christian worldviews, we have a major job to do if we are to help people *want* to find out about Jesus. You can preach all you like (and I am very committed to clear biblical preaching), but if people are not listening we must consider what can be done to encourage them to *want* to pay attention.

The other mistake is to think that positive deconstruction is all that is needed. I don't believe that this one approach is the answer to all our problems in evangelism. For too long Christians have been seeking that particular holy grail. In the 1970s we thought the solution could be in "ungagging God"; if only we could "get the gospel in," people would flock to become Christians. But they didn't. In the 1980s we thought the answer could be in "celebration evangelism"; if only people could see us with our hands in the air, they would become Christians. But they didn't. I do not wish to argue that in the 1990s the answer is in "positive deconstruction"; if only we can help them discover the inadequacies of their world-views, they will all become Christians. They won't! There is no simple answer to evangelism.

What we need is a range of gifts, abilities and strategies that can help different people in different ways and at different times. The approach of positive deconstruction is simply one of these—but one which we must develop and utilize if we are even to begin reaching people today.

For many people in today's culture, it is vital that they discover the inadequacies of the views they have adopted. But this must take place within the context of the whole gospel, which centers around God's love for people. If we genuinely love people, we'll want to help them discover the inadequacies of the worldviews they have adopted, but we'll want to assist them and serve them in other ways too. Employing positive deconstruction is just one part of demonstrating God's love for people. If I may take a liberty with 1 Corinthians 13, "If you are an expert in positive deconstruction, but have not love . . ."

I do not believe that positive deconstruction is the simple key that will make evangelism easy. But, if combined with earnest prayer, clear gospel proclamation, reasoned apologetics and genuine relationships demonstrating practical love, positive deconstruction will help us find evangelism slightly less difficult.

4

Where Do I Start?

IF I AM TO HELP PEOPLE who are not interested in looking at Jesus because they are quite happy with what they believe, I must first set about understanding what it is that they believe. I must do everything I can to understand their worldview. Only then will I know what kinds of questions to raise with them.

In the next two chapters I shall try to show how we can do that. In this chapter we'll look at the principles involved, and in chapter five I will illustrate with a specific example. It is important to note, however, that these two chapters will tell you nothing about how to use positive deconstruction in a conversation with a non-Christian. That will come in chapters six and seven. Chapters four and five are simply about the preparation process—the study we need to do ourselves, so that we can then help non-Christians rethink their beliefs.

This preparation is important, as missionaries have known for years. If God called you to be a missionary in another culture, you wouldn't just hop on a plane and get started. Instead, you would begin by learning about the culture and its worldview—what the people believe, why they believe it, and how you might be able to help them to turn from false beliefs to the truth which is found through Jesus. This would take time and effort on your part. If the place to which you were going contained a mixture of cultures, you would need to get to grips with each of them, and that would take even longer.

It is important to recognize that today's Western world presents tne same challenge that many missionaries have faced for years. We are currently living in a situation demanding multicrosscultural mission.

Now, of course, most of us can't take time out to learn about all the worldviews that surround us. Many of us must learn as we get on with evangelism day by day. But if we are serious about reaching people with the gospel, we must also be serious about studying the worldviews that have been absorbed by the people we are trying to help.

This chapter offers an approach which I find helpful as I attempt to do this.

The Process of Positive Deconstruction

The process of doing positive deconstruction involves four elements: identifying the underlying worldview, analyzing it, affirming the elements of truth which it contains and, finally, discovering its errors.

1. Identifying the worldview. Most people seem unaware of the worldviews they have absorbed, which now underlie their beliefs and values. That is why it is so rare for people to articulate a worldview. Normally they will simply express a belief or live in a certain way without knowing or even thinking about the worldview from which their belief or behavior derives.

Many students tell me they are not interested in hearing about Jesus. But few of them say, "That's because I'm an existentialist," or "That's because I'm a scientific materialist." Generally, they are not at all aware of the underlying philosophies they have adopted.

They reveal these philosophies by the statements they make, but they seem largely oblivious to them.

For instance, many students say to me, "There's nothing wrong with having sex with my girlfriend [or boyfriend]. There can't be anything wrong with something that comes naturally."

When I ask them why they say that, and in particular if they know where this belief comes from, it is only rarely that students know they are expressing a belief which comes from the underlying worldview of naturalism (as we shall see in chapter seven).

At the same time, most Christians are not aware of the worldviews underlying the ideas of people we are trying to reach. All too often we work at a surface level, reacting to individual statements or behavior instead of endeavoring to respond to an underlying philosophy.

Quite often, when I have sought to teach other Christians about a currently influential worldview, some have said, "I don't know anyone who holds that view." But when I give them examples of the kinds of beliefs or behavior that stem from this worldview (that is, the types of things people will say or do if they have absorbed it), their attitude changes.

For instance, I was recently teaching a group of Christians about paganism. One objected that she didn't have any friends who were pagans, so this wouldn't help her. I asked her if she knew people who say that they are not Christians but that they do believe in spirituality.

Yes, she knew plenty of people like that.

And did she know any who would say that organized religion has mucked up our true original spirituality, so we need to rediscover an earlier spirituality?

Yes, some of them said that.

And did any of them believe that, as we develop our spirituality, we must do whatever comes naturally, as long as we don't hurt anyone?

Yes, again, some of them lived that way.

"Well," I said, "these people have absorbed elements of a pagan worldview."

She hadn't realized, and no doubt most of the others in the group hadn't either, that this underlying worldview is where these ideas came from. That night she saw how important it is to understand the underlying worldview. She had been responding to the surface and not the foundation—to the effect and not the cause.

The first task in the process of positive deconstruction, then, is to identify the underlying worldview. This requires us to have a grasp of a wide range of worldviews. We cannot find something if we don't know what we are looking for. Essentially this is a "pattern-matching" process. I have in my mind a large number of contemporary worldviews and know the kinds of beliefs and values to which they lead. Then I consider the beliefs and values being expressed by a person (or in a book or a film), and I look for the best match (or selection of matches) to identify the underlying worldview or worldviews.

Of course, this isn't easy, since it requires us to be familiar with a large number of contemporary worldviews, and most of us aren't. It may seem strange, but the fact is that, although we are surrounded by many different worldviews, most of us don't know what they are. A major reason for this stems from the fact that most of us don't come across them in any pure or easily identifiable form. In chapter two we saw that most individuals hold a reduced and combined mixture of worldviews because of the ways in which they adopt them. Now we shall see that popular culture itself contains a similar mixture because of the ways in which they develop, pass into and circulate around the culture.

In the past, worldviews have usually stemmed from academic institutions or their equivalent. Here clear thinkers (from Plato to Marx, from Descartes to Feuerbach) have developed new ideas, or combinations of ideas, in a fairly pure form. From there the worldviews may trickle down slowly into educational establishments, and then into the media, which popularize them into the culture. Or (increasingly) they may simply leap into the culture through the media. Either way, as they are popularized, the pure worldviews tend to become reduced and combined with others.

Assorted bits of worldviews tend to be utilized and combined with bits of others as they are absorbed into popular culture. In turn, this popular culture feeds the media, and a circle develops in which mixed-up, reduced and combined worldviews are reported and recycled, without much re-analysis at the higher level.

I said this happened "in the past," because recently the process of the development and spread of new worldviews has become even more complicated. Some new ideas, or combinations of ideas, still originate in academic institutions or their equivalent. But increasingly they also originate in television production studios, fashion houses or recording studios, or within club culture or on the street. People living and working at this level thus both shape and are shaped by the culture as they create a fertile ground for the development and spread of new ideas. When this happens, the academics are reduced to observing and analyzing new ideas rather than originating them. (See figure 2.)

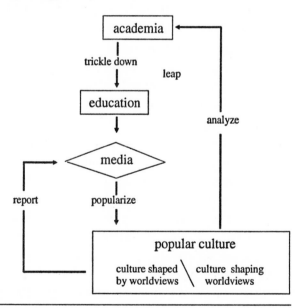

Figure 2. The Development and Spread of Worldviews

This dual origin and development of worldviews tends to lead to a complexity in contemporary culture and to some interesting anomalies. For instance, as I write this book, two very different worldviews are being developed and popularized from the two different sources. Academia and ground level seem to be diametrically opposed. Let me explain.

Currently a lot of academic work is being published[1] which seeks to demonstrate a purely physiological explanation for consciousness (or the soul). This seems to develop and justify a materialistic worldview with no recognition of the supernatural or any spiritual dimension. At the same time, however, a very different worldview is being developed and popularized at ground level. As I write, three of the books on the "top ten" list are centered on claims of the paranormal, the television series *The X-Files* is riding high in the ratings, and every Saturday evening, in the U.K., Mystic Meg gives her predictions about the national lottery. As academics are seeking to develop and popularize materialism, others are pulling in the opposite direction. If we are to engage meaningfully with people in contemporary culture, therefore, we must begin by extracting and identifying the underlying worldviews.

This isn't going to be easy. It is not possible for all of us to have a full understanding of all existing worldviews. We can, however, begin to develop an initial understanding of some of the most influential. And resources are being set up to help us all to find this slightly less difficult.

2. Analyzing the worldview. Once we have identified a particular worldview, we can move on to the next step: analyzing it.

Essentially, we have to ask, "Is it true?" To do this I find it best to employ the three standard philosophical tests of truth—the coherence, correspondence and pragmatic tests. This means that basically I ask three questions: Does it cohere? (That is, does it make sense?) Does it correspond with reality? Does it work? Let's look at each of these in turn.

Does it cohere? This question derives from the theory which holds that if a statement is true, it will cohere. That is, truth will make sense. It will not contain logical inconsistencies or elements that are mutually contradictory. Something that is incoherent cannot be true. It cannot be true if it doesn't make sense.

Let me give you an example of a statement that will fail this coherence test. Suppose I told you that I don't believe in astrology, because I was born under the star sign of Aquarius and Aquarians don't believe in that sort of thing. Do you see how this statement contradicts itself? It is logically inconsistent. As a statement, it doesn't make sense. So it cannot be true.

Does it correspond with reality? This question derives from the theory that if a statement is true, it will correspond with reality. That is, truth properly describes the real world and does not make claims inconsistent with reality.

Here's an example of statements that fail this correspondence test. Mormons believe that Christopher Columbus was not the first person to discover America. They claim that, hundreds of years before Christ, a group of people led by a man named Lehi traveled there from the Middle East and founded a great civilization including such people as the Nephites and Lamanites. This story is coherent on its own terms. It does not, however, seem to describe the real world. I am not aware of any evidence that such a civilization ever existed. It is a great story, but its claims simply do not correspond with reality.

Does it work? This statement derives from the theory that if a statement is true, it will work. That is, truth enables us to function, whereas error does not.

The story is told of a politician, a vicar and a Boy Scout who were traveling together in a plane. Suddenly the engines failed. The pilot bailed out, leaving only two parachutes among the three of them. Immediately the politician said, "I'm the most important, most intelligent person on this plane, so I'm taking one of the parachutes." And grabbing the nearest pack, he jumped out.

The vicar turned to the Boy Scout and said, "You take the other parachute and save yourself. I'm not afraid to die."

"But you don't need to," replied the Boy Scout, "because the most important, most intelligent person on this plane just jumped out with my backpack on."

No matter how much the politician believed that the backpack was a parachute, he would soon find out that it wouldn't work. So his belief wasn't true. If it doesn't work, it can't be true. These three theories of truth and the questions which derive from them provide us with a structured means of analyzing a worldview. They give us a framework of three crucial questions we can ask.

It is important that we use all three of them, because each one on its own is not sufficient. If a statement fails one of these tests, we know that it cannot be true. If it passes just one or two, it is not true. It needs to pass all three.

Not everything that coheres is true. My little daughter tells some wonderfully coherent stories about how somebody else must have come and put the dirty marks on the wallpaper or broken that vase. The tales make sense, but they aren't true.

Not everything that corresponds with the reality that we see is necessarily true. For thousands of years people believed that the sun orbits the earth. That was what they saw. It corresponded with their perception of reality. But it was not true.

Not everything that works is true. I knew a doctor who gave bright red vitamin tablets to a patient with a recurrent complaint and told her that they were a new, expensive treatment that was bound to solve her problem. She got completely better. The "medicine" had worked, but it was not true that it was a medicine. Scientists would have called it a placebo.

When we look at any worldview, then, we need to ask all three questions about it. Does it make sense? Does it correspond with reality? Does it work? As we do so, we can look for elements of truth that we may affirm as well as errors that we can discover.

Let me explain what this means.

3. Affirming the truth. Many of us are uncomfortable with the idea that any non-Christian worldview might contain truth. Somehow the notion that we don't have a monopoly on truth seems to threaten us. It is much easier for us to believe that others are totally wrong and that we are totally right. But this is simply not the case. Non-Christian worldviews are not totally wrong. They do contain elements of truth (sometimes very large), and we must affirm them. If we fail to do so, people will not listen to us, and why should they? No one wants to be worked over by an arrogant bigot. On the other hand, as we shall see later, people will engage in discussion with someone who is on their side, also seeking after truth.

But there is another reason it is vitally important that we affirm the truth in other worldviews. And this has nothing to do with reaching others; it is to stop us from backing off into error ourselves. Whether we like it or not, other worldviews contain truth. If we reject them totally, we shall find that, as well as rejecting error, we are also rejecting truth. And if we reject truth, we push ourselves into error. Here's an example.

Historically, Christians have followed the way of Jesus and have been intimately involved not just in proclaiming the message of love, but also in demonstrating it by social action. Around the beginning of the twentieth century, however, this changed, and the church temporarily lost its social conscience. Why was that? It was partly due to a reaction against theological liberalism, which reduced the value of the Bible and increased the importance of social action. Instead of just rejecting part of theological liberalism (the devaluation of the Bible), many Christians rejected all of liberalism's insights and consequently rejected social action. If only we had affirmed the elements of truth that liberalism maintained, we would not have thrown out the social-action baby with the biblical-criticism bath water.

If we are not going to push ourselves into error, we must affirm truth wherever it is, knowing that ultimately all truth is God's truth and all worldviews contain elements of this truth.

4. Discovering the error. As well as containing truth, however, non-Christian worldviews also contain error. Jesus makes exclusive claims. If these claims are true, alternative worldviews cannot be totally true.

When we analyze a worldview using the three criteria of truth, we are attempting not only to affirm truth but also to discover those errors. We may find that a particular worldview is not coherent, or that it doesn't correspond with reality, or that it will not work, or indeed any combination of these. This, of course, is where we are aiming. It is a prerequisite that we identify the worldview; it is necessary for us to analyze it; it is valuable for us to affirm the truth that it contains; but it is also vital that we discover its error. Only then shall we be able to help people see this error for themselves so that they will become uncomfortable with their current view and begin looking at Jesus.

Uncomfortable for Us Too

Thinking through a non-Christian worldview can take a long time and can be quite a disturbing press. I often find that I go through three phases as I subject a new worldview to positive deconstruction.

Initially, I may have an emotional reaction born of ignorance. Sometimes I catch myself thinking, *What a load of rubbish! How can anyone believe this?* I am not alone in this. It is a common reaction among Christians, and unfortunately it is often due to the fact that we have read not the source material but just someone else's biased summary of it. Thus we are actually reacting not to the worldview itself but to a caricature of it. Sadly, some do not get beyond this stage; they seem only to ridicule other people's genuine and sincerely held beliefs.

I can move out of this phase only by finding out about the particular belief. So I set about reading the source documents and talking to people who hold this worldview or elements of it. When I do this, I begin to find that it is not such a load of rubbish after all. I begin to understand their arguments. It starts to make sense. It may even begin to sound convincing. Sometimes I get a sinking feeling as I wonder whether they might actually be right after all—perhaps I should give up my faith. Again, unfortunately, some Christians reach this stage and do not move through it. They either give up being Christians or put on Christian blinkers, refusing to think about anyone else's beliefs again, and certainly deciding never to engage in personal evangelism any more. "It disturbs my own faith too much," they say.

Finally, I step back, and, having understood the worldview, I set about subjecting it to positive deconstruction. I usually sit down with a work sheet (as shown in figure 3) and work carefully through the worldview. I ask the three questions, and for each one I write down what truth I can affirm and what error I can discover. (The next chapter will give an example of this as we use the worksheet as a framework for subjecting relativism to positive deconstruction.) As I do this, I usually have a series of what psychologists call "Aha!" experiences. Light dawns on particular aspects of the worldview, and, while I find truths to affirm, I also discover errors. At last I move into the final phase, where I am able to respond to the worldview intelligently and fairly.

Identify: _____

Analyze:

	Affirm truth	Discover error
1. Cohere?		
2. Correspond?		
3. Work?		

Figure 3. Positive Deconstruction Worksheet

I Know It Isn't Easy

When I have spoken about this process at conferences or training courses, occasionally some have said, "I'm not sure I could ever understand this, let alone do it. Does that mean I can't be effective in evangelism?"

The answer is no.

The fact is that if we genuinely want to be available for God to use in reaching others, he will use us—whatever knowledge we have. If you were to hop on a plane right now and go to a culture you don't understand, God could use you in that situation. But you would be of much more use if you first set about understanding the culture and the worldviews that underlie it. Of course, that isn't easy. Preparing missionaries to go overseas never has been easy. Nowadays, those of us who stay at home and want to reach people here are facing the same difficult task.

Understanding the many and varied complex ideas and philosophies in today's world is going to be difficult. It is far simpler to learn how to sing a song or act a sketch. But it must be done. This is especially true for those of us who want to reach today's young people. Gone are the days (if they ever were) when to be effective in youth ministry all you needed to know was how to give your testimony and how to play ping-pong. Today, among many other things, we need to be able to understand and respond to a wide range of worldviews. This is difficult, but if we won't do it I fear we will fail a whole generation.

5

It's Not
for Me

SO MUCH FOR THE THEORY. Now let's apply the process to a real example. In this chapter we'll consider how to apply positive deconstruction to a very popular and pervasive view: relativism. In order to explain this, I shall use some real examples from my conversations with other people. It is, however, important to realize that at this stage I am still giving you a desk exercise: we will be thinking about how to subject this worldview to positive deconstruction for ourselves. Only in chapter six will we move on to the question of how to use this approach to help real people who hold these views.

You may find it helpful to draw up a worksheet like the one in figure 3 and use it as we go through the four stages of positive deconstruction. I do this whenever I come across any new worldview.

Stage 1: Identify. Very rarely do I meet people who tell me that they are relativists. Almost every day, however, I talk with people who make relativistic statements. They say such things as these:

"It may be true for you, but it isn't true for me."

"You can't say that is wrong; it might be wrong for you, but it's right for me."

"Missionaries shouldn't try to convert people. If people are happy with what they believe, leave them alone."

Each of these statements derives from the underlying philosophy of relativism.

Relativism is the name given to the idea that everything is relative (by which I don't mean Auntie Gladys!). It is the belief that there are no absolutes—no absolute truth, no absolute right or wrong, in fact no absolute anything. To the relativist (someone who believes in relativism), everything is relative; it depends upon who you are, where you are, what you are, when you are, and so on. Truth is relative, morality is relative, religion is relative—everything is relative. A belief can be true for me but false for you; a decision can be right for you but wrong for me. Danish philosopher Søren Kierkegaard put it this way: "The thing is to find a truth which is true for me." More recently, British theologian Don Cupitt has said, "Capital T truth is dead . . . truth is plural, socially conditioned and perpetually changing."

These philosophical and theological ideas have trickled down into our culture, which is now almost wholly relativistic. A recent survey, published as *The Invisible Generation,* revealed that 70 percent of young people believe that absolute truth does not exist and that all truth is relative and personal.

Although many people accept relativism, however, most do not know what it is. This isn't a philosophy that they have thoughtfully considered and then accepted. It is simply one in which they are immersed day by day as they learn from relativistic teachers, read relativistic magazines and watch relativistic television. Relativism, then, has become so internalized that it is not just something people believe, but simply the way in which they think.

Stages 2-4: Analyze, affirm truth and discover error. Let's analyze relativism according to the three tests of truth and, at each stage, see what truth we can affirm and what error we can discover.

1. Is relativism coherent?

Does relativism cohere? That is, does it make sense, or is it logically inconsistent?

I wish I could find truth to affirm here. Some of the most intelligent people I meet and debate with are relativists. It is very embarrassing if I am drawn to say that I find the whole basis of their view incoherent. But I do.

When people tell me that they believe there is no such thing as absolute truth, I have to work very hard to resist asking them if they are sure about that (which they usually are), and if they are, whether they are absolutely sure (which they often are). In effect, they are saying, "It is absolutely true that there is no such thing as absolute truth." When people state, "There is no such thing as absolute truth," they are making a statement which itself is absolute. So one cannot even state relativism without denying it. The whole idea of relativism does not make sense. It disappears upon its own hypothesis.

But the problem is worse than that. Relativism denies a fundamental principle of logic known as Aristotle's principle of noncontradiction. You may never have heard of this principle or realized how important it is. But it is the foundation of the logic we use day by day, and if we get rid of it, we really are in trouble. Basically, Aristotle's principle says that a statement cannot be both true and false at the same time. Although complementary truth claims can be true, contradictory truth claims cannot. For example, I could make two truth claims about the desk on which I am currently writing. I could say, "This is a piece of furniture" and "This is a desk." These truth claims are different, but they can both be true. They are complementary; they give two different bits of information which can both be true. But suppose I make two mutually exclusive truth claims: "This is made of wood" and "This is not made of wood." These beliefs cannot both be true. They contradict each other. If one is true, the other cannot be. This desk cannot be made of wood and not made of wood at the same time. In order to accept relativism, one has to abandon this fundamental principle of logic and everything based upon it. One has to be prepared to say that something can be true and not true at the same time: it all depends upon who you are, where you are, when you are and so on. Therefore, not only is relativism in itself incoherent, but also, to accept it, we have to lose the solid basis for all logic. That is the road to madness.

2. Does relativism correspond with reality?

Let's now consider whether relativism corresponds with the real world in which we live. Is the world around us wholly relativistic, or are there clear absolutes?

Here, I find that there are some true elements I can affirm. There are certain statements that can be true for one person but not true for another. Let me give you a couple of examples, from the areas of aesthetics and ethics.

My wife, Carol, thinks I am gorgeous. She will tell you that she thinks I am the most lovable, kissable person in the world. Other women probably wouldn't agree (at least I hope not). The statement "Nick is gorgeous" is true for her but not true for other people. In some ways, that's the way the world is. There are many different opinions and preferences, from colors to football teams, which are true for one person but not true for another.

In a slightly different way, there are also some ethical decisions which can be different for different people at different times. One may believe that taking things from other people is wrong, but then realize that taking the gun from a bank robber is right. Clearly, in this case, it does depend on the circumstances. Even those of us who believe in a prescriptive ethic, based on God's revelation in the Bible, also recognize the importance of context in applying God's absolutes in this fallen world. For example, in the Old Testament we find the story of Rahab, who was apparently rewarded by God for telling a lie when she said the spies were not with her (Josh 2). She was later praised as one of the great heroes of faith (Heb 11:31). In the New Testament, the question of eating food sacrificed to idols depended upon what the individual believed about it (1 Cor 8).

The Truth in Relativism

We make a mistake, then, if in rejecting relativism we fail to perceive and affirm the truth it contains. Doing so would simply be to push ourselves into dogmatism. It is not true to say that everything is absolute: context and individual circumstances are important.

But even though there are these elements of truth to affirm and insights to value, it doesn't take long to discover that the fundamental principle of relativism does not correspond to reality. The world in which we live is not without absolutes; everything is not relative. There are many things that are true for all people at all times and in all places. They are absolutely true.

Let me demonstrate this with an illustration. I often have conversations with students which go something like this:

Student: God is OK for you. He helps you because you believe in him. But he's not for me. He doesn't exist for me, because I don't believe in him.

Me: Sorry, I'm not quite clear. Are you saying that God exists for me because I believe in him, but he doesn't exist for you because you don't believe in him?

Student: Yes, that's exactly what I'm saying: God exists for you, but he doesn't exist for me.

Me: I can see that's a very appealing belief, but I'm not really sure if it could be possible.

Student: Why not?

Me: Well, think with me about the way the world is.

Student: What do you mean?

Me: Do you see that wall over there? Do you think that wall could exist for me but not exist for you, so that you could walk straight through it?

Student: No, of course it couldn't.

Me: Do you see this floor here?

Student: Yes.

Me: Do you think it could exist for me, but not exist for you, so that you'd fall straight through it?

Student: No, of course it couldn't.

Me: Why is it, then, that you think God could exist for me but not exist for you? Isn't it the case that either God exists or he doesn't? How could he exist for me but not exist for you?

The plain fact is that we live in a world in which there *are* absolute truths. Many statements are either true or not true. I may say that Southampton Football Club is the best team to support, and that might be true for me but not true for you. But if I say that Southampton Football Club is going to win the cup this year, that is either true or not true. Either Southampton will win the cup or it won't. It can't be true for me and not true for you. That's the way the world is. We don't create our own reality; we respond to a real world out there.

It does not therefore correspond with reality to say that there is no such thing as absolute truth and that all truth is relative. There are absolutes. We are surrounded by them day by day, and we ignore them at our peril.

3. Does relativism work?

Finally, let's consider whether relativism works. If people took their relativism seriously and really believed that there was no such thing as absolute truth, what kind of life would they lead?

To begin with, there are truths to affirm here. Those who take a relativistic approach to life have developed and emphasized certain insights which are obviously valuable. For instance, they have been keen to draw the distinction between "personal" and "propositional" truth. They argue that truth that is expressed in propositions is not as important as truth that is known and lived personally. There is much here that I would wish to affirm. Propositions on their own can be cold and hard, whereas we are real people who need not just to know but also to experience truth.

When I write the statement "Nick loves Carol" in the sand at the beach, this is a truth expressed in a proposition. But it has an effect upon Carol only because she knows that I am not just saying it as a proposition; it is also personally true. She lives it and experiences it. Having said that, however, it has the capacity to be personally true only because it is also propositionally true. If my statement were a lie, no matter how much she believed it, she could never experience that personal truth. At best, she could have only an illusion. Clearly, we need propositional truth. Relativists move into an illusory world if they say we don't. But we also need personal truth, which is that propositional truth applied in our lives. I want to affirm relativism's insight into the importance of this fact.

There is, however, clear error in the relativistic position, which can be discovered by questioning whether it works. Relativists must face major problems if they seek to live out their creed. Let me give you two examples, in the areas of knowledge and ethics.

Once I spent a long time talking to the principal of a high school at which I was speaking. He told me that he didn't accept Aristotle's principle of noncontradiction; he believed that there was no such thing as absolute truth. As I drove home, I began to wonder how on earth he could mark his students' exam papers. How could he tell a student that her answers were wrong, since he believes that there is no absolute right or wrong? What would he say to the student who replied, "These answers might be wrong for you, but they are right for me," or "For you the capital of France may be Paris, but for me it's Bognor Regis"? In rejecting absolute truth, don't relativists also reject all possibility of any absolute body of knowledge? Everything becomes relative, and they are reduced to talking about a consensus of what most people believe.

The problem becomes even greater in the field of ethics, since the stakes are much higher. Here we are talking not about exam answers but about people's lives. If there is no absolute truth, there is also no absolute right or wrong. It all depends upon who you are, where you are, when you are. What could a relativist say to Hitler? He can't say that killing six million Jews was wrong, but only that he believes it would be wrong for him. Who is to say whether it was right or wrong for Hitler?

Although relativism has produced some helpful insights, then, we can also see that it is actually unlivable. That is why one can never actually find a complete relativist. Even those who claim to be relativists base their lives on some absolutes. They believe that some things are absolutely true or false, and some things are absolutely right or wrong; they couldn't live their lives any other way.

How Did You Get On?

If you have followed this reasoning with me, you may find that

Identify: Relativism

Analyze:

	Affirm truth	Discover error
1. Cohere?		"All truth is relative" is an absolute statement Can't state relativism without denying it
2. Correspond?	Some things true for different people —opinions (e.g., best football team) Some things true at different times —take gun from bank robber —lie to save people (e.g., Rahab)	*Not* true that there are no absolutes (e.g., floor/wall/God exists for everyone or for no one) —can't exist for one and not for others
3. Work?	Personal and not just propositional truth —need to experience and not just know truth	But what about . . . 1. Knowledge —no body of knowledge (e.g., mark exam papers) —"wrong"/"right" for me 2. Ethics —nothing absolutely wrong (e.g., Hitler—right for him)

Figure 4. Positive Deconstruction of Relativism

your worksheet looks something like figure 4. Don't worry if yours looks different; you may have thought of other truths to affirm or errors to discover. Also, don't be concerned if you found this very difficult and could grasp only some of my points. You can still be effective in evangelism even if you don't see the implications of all the arguments in this chapter. You don't need to know how to subject relativism to the process of positive deconstruction totally in order to be able to help people who have adopted it as a worldview. Even if you have understood just one error of this worldview, that may be all that some people need in order to make them think again and be prepared to look at Jesus.

It is important that we don't lose sight of the objective of positive deconstruction. It isn't to fill in all the boxes on the worksheet with every single truth that can be affirmed and error that can be discovered. Rather, it is to understand enough about a worldview to enable us to awaken within a non-Christian a heart response that says, "I am not sure that what I believe is right after all. I want to find out more about Jesus." For some people, this may require a long, in-depth analysis, while for others it may simply take one comment. And each of us will be able to provide help at some level.

Let's now look at how we can put the principle of positive deconstruction into practice.

6

But They
Won't Listen!

WE'VE DONE OUR MISSIONARY training, and we've understood
an underlying worldview. We're now ready to help non-Christians
who are not interested in hearing about Jesus because they are quite
happy with their current beliefs. How are we going to do this? How
do we put our positive deconstruction into practice?

We noted in chapter two the beginnings of the development of a
postmodern culture. We shall now see the implications of this for
how (and why) we should help people engage in a positive deconstruction of their worldview.

There are those, even some Christians, who would vigorously
disagree with my last sentence. They argue that we must accept the
conclusions of this increasingly postmodern culture and give up on
any concept of worldview or, indeed, rationality. They say that
worldview is dead and people no longer think. Therefore, they
argue, it is pointless for us to try to help people think about their

worldview, since they no longer have one; they just live life on the surface and we must find a way of relating to that.

I am certain that such a sellout to postmodernism is a great mistake. People do have worldviews, and they will continue to hold them. As we have already noted, when we were thinking about postmodernism, the worldviews that people hold are selected on a "mix-and-match" basis. They are muddled up and inconsistent. But they are still there. Similarly, people still think. We are rational beings. Some postmodern theoreticians may argue for the death of rationality (although, strangely, they do this in a rational way). If we are created in the image of God, however, all of us, Christian or non-Christian, modern or postmodern, will continue to think.[1] So we cannot accept the speculative conclusions of postmodernism.

Yet we can (and must) work within the methodology of postmodernism if we really are going to reach people in this culture. Two major characteristics of postmodernism are of particular importance to us in evangelism: (1) the emphasis on questioning and (2) the displacement of propositional truth in favor of stories. If we are to be effective within this postmodern culture, then, our evangelism must involve the appropriate use of questions and stories. That is not actually anything new; it is the way in which Jesus taught. He made use of questions, often answering one question with another. And he told the greatest stories of all time.

We shall return to the use of stories in chapter ten, but in this chapter we will look particularly at the use of questions.

Postmodernism questions everything, even the questions themselves. Deconstruction goes hand in glove with postmodernism. Deconstruction as employed by postmodernism, however, is somewhat negative. Ideas, beliefs, even sentences and words, are taken apart until one is left with nothing. Our task, it seems to me, is to encourage that deconstruction, but to help people to see that it can be positive, such that it is possible to arrive at something firm and good. Let's consider, now, how we can do that.

No matter how clearly we may understand the inadequacies of a particular worldview, we can't expect people who currently hold that view to recognize these inadequacies just because we speak about them. But we can encourage people to engage in the postmodern activity of questioning everything. We can help people to think through their beliefs and values thoroughly—and thus to discover the inadequacies for themselves. Our role is to demonstrate genuine love for them by being there, and serving them, as they think through their worldview at their own speed. Our role is not to abuse them by rudely seeking to impose our conclusion upon them at our speed.

It Takes Time

It is bound to take people time, sometimes a very long time, to perceive the inadequacies of a particular worldview. Think back to the last chapter. I don't know how long it took you to understand it. But I wouldn't be surprised if you had to read some sections two or three times. Even then, perhaps you had to sit back and reflect on the information you had taken in before you were able to see the inadequacies of relativism. This isn't due to any weakness on your part (or, I hope, to my failure as an author, though that is more likely). Rather, it is inevitable, given the fact that whenever we think through complex ideas it takes time for them to fall into place. We don't understand them immediately; we have to wait for that moment when it all suddenly seems to make sense for us.

In the same way, we must give non-Christians the time and space they require. Indeed, they need this even more than we do, since, for them, it is not a purely theoretical or academic question we are inviting them to consider. For we are asking them to rethink some fundamental, underlying beliefs and assumptions upon which they have based their lives until now. This is a disturbing experience for them, and if we try to push them too fast it can be traumatic. If our positive deconstruction is to be truly positive, we must give people the time they need so they can take it at a pace with which they are comfortable.

In practical terms this means, in fact, rethinking our goals in evangelism.

I spend a lot of my time away from home carrying out university missions. Sometimes, when I return, well-meaning Christians ask me, "How many people were converted?" But that is the wrong question, and I'm afraid it shows how out of touch they are with today's generation. Many of the students I am seeking to help day by day are nowhere near ready to become Christians. Nor do they even want to hear about Jesus; they are quite happy with their own views, thank you very much. With these people my immediate goal is not to see them become Christians (although that would be a marvelous miracle of God, and indeed I have sometimes seen it). Nor is it even to see them take one step closer to Jesus; often we are not quite in that ball park either. My goal is just to help them to take one step further away from their current worldview.

One Small Step
Let me give you an example. I remember two young women in the college where I carried out my very first mission. They came to every event, listening to what I said and engaging in the debates. One of them was already very positive about the gospel, and toward the end of the week she prayed to commit her life to Christ. The other was nowhere near that point, and she said at the end of the week, "I don't want to become a Christian, but I am now less of an atheist than I was before." That was successful evangelism. She hadn't become a Christian, nor could I even say that she had taken a step closer to Jesus, but she had taken a step further away from her current worldview.

We must have a much wider definition of evangelism than just inviting people to respond to Jesus, or even just talking to them about Jesus. When I sit in a student room listening to Nirvana, and I open up a discussion on Kurt Cobain's struggle with the emptiness of life, that is evangelism. When I ask a student to have a drink with me in the bar and tell me why he believes we are purely physical, with no spiritual nature or significance, and what difference this scientific materialist worldview makes in his life, that too is evangelism. I may not have called him to respond to Jesus or even mentioned the name of Jesus. But it's all part of the long, slow evangelistic process that enables people who are currently comfortable with their worldviews to become uncomfortable with them, and therefore open to looking at Jesus—but without becoming unnecessarily traumatized in the process.

I understand that some Christians will feel unsettled by this approach. Indeed, quite often, when I explain my ministry, some tell me that I should "just tell them they are wrong." They seem to think all we've got to do is to tell people the truth and they will immediately agree with us. But that is not the way it is. Usually, people will not even listen to what we say, let alone accept it. Neither should we really expect them to do so. People are individuals, created in the image of God, with the ability to think for themselves and to make their own decisions. If God has given people free will, who are we to try to take it away from them? Instead, our role is to work in partnership with them, stimulating them to think again about what they believe and being there to serve them as they do.

We need to be clear about what it means to educate people, whether about the inadequacies of non-Christian worldviews or about the truth of the claims of Christ. Evangelism involves a large element of education. So if we are to develop a good approach to evangelism, it is important to understand the Christian approach to education. Let's now quickly look at a Christian model for education and then apply that to evangelism, specifically in the area of positive deconstruction.

How Can We Tell People Anything?

In the world of education, teachers don't teach in just any way they want to. They follow a particular model or theory of education. In recent years there has been a tension between two different models: the didactic method (sometimes called "teacher-centered teaching") and the critical method (sometimes called "student-centered learning"). The tension has been mirrored in the church, as some Christians argue for the adoption of the critical method in our Christian teaching while others call for a return to what they see as the more traditional didactic model.

I believe, however, that if we look beyond these models to the assumptions about the nature of knowledge upon which they are based, we shall find that actually neither is authentically Christian. Rather, we need to build a different model of education, which is founded upon a Christian view of knowledge and which can then serve as the basis upon which we carry out our Christian teaching, and thus our evangelism.

The didactic model of education is sometimes called "teacher-centered teaching" because it is based on the body of knowledge which the teacher holds and which she delivers to the student. According to this approach, the teacher speaks and the student listens, so information goes from the teacher to the student. On a practical level, this usually means that students sit in rows listening to the teacher and taking notes in an attempt to remember the information she has given them.

By contrast, the application of the critical method is sometimes called "student-centered learning" because it is based on the students, who explore, question and formulate truth for themselves. On a practical level, this means that students work on their own or in groups, investigating, discussing and debating.

The critical method is often thought to be a modern development which has superseded the more traditional didactic model. This is not strictly the case, since its roots go back at least as far as Socrates. In the world of education, however, this model certainly rose to prominence in the 1960s and 1970s, before the move back toward the didactic model in more recent years.

This swing between two models has been reflected in the church. When schools were adopting the critical method, churches were developing home groups and discussion groups. Later, as some in education began to call for a return to the didactic model, some in the church began to call for a return to "preaching it straight." Consequently, there is now a tension among Christians between the two models of education. On one side are those who argue that Christian education must adopt the critical method. Some hold this view from a commitment to this theory of education, and others for more pragmatic reasons, pointing out that today's generation have been brought up with this method (they are not used to sitting and listening) and so will be reached only in this way. On the other side are those who point out that we are called to rescue people from the ungodly aspects of our culture, and they include the critical method in that category. So they argue for a return to the didactic model in our Christian teaching.

Faced with these two models, how are we to proceed? If Christian approaches to education have merely mirrored those in the world, we must be deeply suspicious that something is wrong. A way forward is provided by taking the analysis one stage deeper. The two models of education are actually based on two different understandings of the nature of knowledge (that is, two different epistemologies). I believe that neither of these is actually a Christian view of knowledge. Therefore, it is inappropriate for us to adopt either of the two models; nor should we even attempt some kind of Hegelian[2] synthesis.

The didactic model stems from a dogmatic view of knowledge, the underlying assumption being that truth is something that one person can hold and transmit to someone else. A teacher adopting this model is essentially saying, "I know the truth, and I shall tell you what it is." Thus the teacher places himself in a position of authority. Ultimately, he determines truth.

The critical method, by contrast, stems from a relativistic view of knowledge, the underlying assumption being that there is no absolute truth. The teacher adopting this model is essentially saying, "I know no absolute truth to tell you, but I'll help you find the truth that is true for you." Thus the student is placed in a position of authority. Ultimately, he formulates his own truth.

Neither of these underlying epistemologies actually reflects the Christian view of knowledge. It follows that we cannot accept either of the educational models which derive from them. Instead, we need to consider the Christian view of knowledge and then build on that a Christian model of education (and then a model for evangelism).

What then is the Christian view of knowledge?

It is evident that a Christian cannot be a relativist, because one of the central claims of Christ is that he actually is the Truth (Jn 14:6). We cannot formulate truth for ourselves; truth is something that God creates and reveals. At the same time, a Christian cannot be a dogmatist, since God has not fully revealed all his truth to us (Deut 29:29). Indeed, our understanding of what he has revealed is limited and flawed by our finite and sinful minds. Therefore, a Christian view of knowledge would seem to be one that recognizes that *absolute truth exists, but that it is only God who holds it.* Truth is determined by God and God alone. Our knowledge of that truth is correct only to the extent that we have correctly understood the amount of God's truth that he has chosen to reveal to us.

Starting from this basis, we can now construct a Christian model of education. This model will be neither teacher-centered nor student-centered but God-centered. God is the authority; he creates and holds truth. Both the teacher and the student are attempting to understand and respond to it. Truth is not determined by the teacher, who communicates it, or by the student, who formulates it. Rather, it is determined by God, who reveals it. And the teacher and student work together to seek after truth and respond to it.

In this model, then, the teacher communicates to the student her understanding of God's revealed truth. This approach has similarities to the didactic model, but it is not in any way dogmatic. For the teacher recognizes that her understanding is incomplete and could be faulty. Therefore, she invites the student to join her in critically assessing both his own understanding of truth and hers.

This approach also has similarities to the critical method, but it is not in any way relativistic. The goal of the critique is not to formulate subjective truth, but to discover God's revealed truth more accurately. The teacher is not aiming to impose her knowledge on the student, nor is the student constructing his own truth. Neither, indeed, are they trying to manufacture some synthesis with which they both feel happy. By contrast, they are together submitting to God as they endeavor to discover, understand and respond to what he has revealed.

Evangelism: Helping People Discover God's Truth

The application of this Christian model of education to evangelism is fairly obvious. I am not there just to tell people straight that they are wrong, but to raise questions with them and to invite them to raise questions with me. We are engaging together in the search for a greater understanding of truth.

My goal is to help them have an "Aha!" experience—they discover for themselves the inadequacies of their adopted world-view—so that they then want to hear about Jesus. They must come to that conclusion themselves, rather than just accepting what I say.

This means that, although I have some information which I want to communicate to them, I want to do it in such a way that I encourage them to think, question and come to their own conclusions. This usually means giving them information in the form of a question rather than a statement. There is no set, pat approach, but I often use phrases such as, "I can see a lot of truth in that, but have you thought about . . . ?" or, "If I held your view, I think one thing that would bug me would be . . ."

At the same time, I must be prepared to change my mind too. I always make this clear to non-Christians with whom I talk. I tell them I am wildly enthusiastic about being a Christian and convinced that the claims of Jesus are true—but I am prepared to change my mind on anything if I can be convinced, by the evidence, that I have got it wrong. I am even prepared to stop being a Christian if I can be convinced that Jesus did not rise from the dead. (That may sound shocking, but it is really no different from what Paul said; see 1 Cor 15:14.) After all, I am asking them to be prepared to change their minds about what they believe, and it is simply not fair for me to ask them to do something I am not prepared to do myself.

Indeed, if we are to take the whole process of positive deconstruction seriously, we must positively deconstruct not only what non-Christians believe, but also what we believe. We shall look at this in some detail in chapter eight, but first let me take a chapter to give you a real-life example of positive deconstruction in practice.

7

If They
Believe This,
They Can't
Believe That

I SPEND A LOT OF TIME hanging around student union lounges, chatting with students. When I ask them if they plan to come to any of the events at which I am speaking, they usually say no, telling me they are not interested because they are quite happy as they are. But I find that if I can get them to talk about what they believe, I am sometimes able to help them think again about whether they really are as happy as they say.

To illustrate positive deconstruction in practice, let me give you an example of a conversation with one particular student; I'll call him Tom. Actually, this is a somewhat edited version of the conversation. The real one naturally wandered around and rambled much more, but I have distilled it to make it more readable.

Tom was clearly a quick, logical thinker, but that doesn't mean that this approach can be used only with people like him. It is just that, for the purposes of this book, the approach is best demonstrated by examples of this sort. Many people will not think as quickly as Tom did, and, for them, one would have to go much more slowly. Others think in a less linear, more intuitive, artistic or practical way, and, for them, one would have to come at it from different angles and in different ways. But this example should give you some idea of positive deconstruction in practice.

The Naturalist

Nick: Are you coming to the open debate at lunchtime?

Tom: No, I'm not interested. I think I'd disagree with everything you say.

Nick: Really? Why is that?

Tom: Because you are so opposed to homosexuals.

Nick: I'm not; what makes you think I am?

Tom: All Christians are. The church is homophobic.

Nick: You're right that the church has often given the impression that you can't be a Christian and a homosexual.

Tom: But isn't that what you believe?

Nick: No, not really. When I look at Jesus, I see someone who welcomes everyone, whatever their sexuality. The only question is whether people should continue in homosexual activity once they have become Christians.

Tom: But why shouldn't they? I'm a homosexual and it's perfectly natural.

Nick: Tell me more. Why do you say that? What do you mean by "natural"?

Tom: Well, I'm a homosexual. That's just the way I am. It's natural for me, so no one can tell me it's wrong.

Nick: I see. What you are saying is that because it comes naturally for you, it can't be wrong.

Tom: Yes, that's it. How could anything that is natural be wrong?

Nick: I can certainly agree with a lot of what you are saying there. And so would many others. Great philosophers, with much better brains than mine, have said the same thing. In fact there is a name for it. It's called "naturalism." That isn't naturism, where you run around with no clothes on, but naturalism, which says that whatever is natural is right. The way that things naturally are is the way things ought to be. So the only criterion we need for deciding whether something is right or not is whether it's natural or not.

Tom: "Well, that's it, then. I'm naturally a homosexual, so no one can tell me that it's wrong. Christians can go and — — themselves.

Nick: Certainly I agree with a lot of what you are saying.

Tom: You do?

Nick: Yes, because so many things that come naturally are clearly right. Love, for instance. It comes naturally to me to love my children, and obviously that is right. And eating comes naturally, so that has got to be right, or we'd die.

Tom: Yeah, that's right.

(At this point some of the Christian students who were with me were getting a bit edgy and wondering if they had booked the right evangelist.)

Nick: But, hang on a minute. There's a problem.

Tom: What's that?

Nick: There are other things that come naturally that I'm not sure we would want to say are right.

Tom: Like what?

Nick: Well, anger, hatred, violence. The poet Tennyson described nature as "red in tooth and claw." Is that the way things should be?

Tom: I suppose it's got to be.

Nick: But are you happy with that? Do you really want to say that everything that comes naturally is right? What if a child abuser says it is natural for him to have sex with five-year-old girls, does that make it right?

Tom: Of course not, but that's not what I'm doing.

Nick: I know you're not. I can see that you would never do anything like that. But the problem is that if we say that homosexuality is right just because it's natural, we've also got to accept that other things are also right just because they are natural. That's where naturalism leads us.

Tom: I'm not so sure about that.

Nick: No, nor am I. Especially when I look at people who took their naturalism to its logical conclusion. The Marquis de Sade, for instance—he was an ethical naturalist who argued that nothing could ever be wrong if it came naturally. He said that because men are naturally stronger than women, it is right for men to use and abuse women in any way they want. If you've got a strong stomach, read his *120 Days of Sodom,* and see where that led him.

Tom: But that doesn't mean that other things that come naturally are wrong. Some natural things are clearly right, and others are clearly wrong.

Nick: Yes, I agree. It's as if our nature has become twisted and mucked up. So there are some things that come naturally that are right and others that are not.

Tom: But we know what those are. We know which things are right and which aren't. I'd never abuse a child. . . . Look, I've just realized what the difference is. An abuser is hurting someone, and the Marquis de Sade hurt people. When I'm having sex with another consenting gay, I'm not hurting anyone. In fact, I'm making two people really happy.

Nick: I think you are quite right.

Tom: You do?

Nick: Well, not as regards whether you are hurting someone when you are having homosexual sex; let's come back to that in a minute. But I think you are right in saying that there is a difference. What we've seen is that naturalism is inadequate as an ethical philosophy—as a means of deciding whether something is right or wrong. It's not enough simply to say that something is right just because it comes naturally. There are too many obviously wrong things that come naturally to too many people. What you are saying now is that the way we can tell whether something is right or wrong is by asking whether it hurts anyone or makes people happy.

Tom: Yes. If it makes people happy and doesn't hurt anyone, it's OK.

Nick: Again, there are great philosophers who would agree with you. In fact, we've shifted ground from naturalism to another philosophy, called "utilitarianism."

Tom: Yes, I've studied something about that in history. It's all about the greatest-happiness principle.

Nick: That's it. Utilitarianism says that something is right if it produces the greatest happiness for the greatest number.

Tom: And being a homosexual makes me happy.

Nick: So you say. And I can understand that. There are many things that make people happy that are obviously right.

Tom: So as long as I'm happy and I'm not hurting anyone, that's OK. It's just a pain when others try to make me feel guilty about it—but that's their problem.

Nick: Of course, there is a problem that we'll have to face.

Tom: What's that?

Nick: It seems OK to say that we can decide whether something is right or not according to whether it makes people happy and doesn't hurt people—until we realize that we don't always know whether something is going to hurt people or not.

Tom: What do you mean?

Nick: Well, I don't know everything—do you? How can I tell whether something that appears OK on the surface might actually be hurting people? Even really intelligent, educated people don't know that. Take doctors, for instance. When my wife Carol and I had our first baby, we were told to lay him on his tummy to sleep. That seemed sensible; he wouldn't choke if he was sick. Doctors thought they were giving good advice that would bring the greatest happiness to the greatest number. But it turned out they'd got it wrong, and laying babies on their tummies made them susceptible to "crib death." You see, they didn't know what would bring the greatest happiness for the greatest number.

Tom: What's that got to do with it?

Nick: Tell me if I'm wrong here, but aren't you making the same mistake as those doctors? You are saying that gay sex isn't hurting anyone, but how do you know?

Tom: But I can see that it isn't.

Nick: Can you? Or is it just that you can't see it *yet?*

Tom: Well, I can't see the future.

Nick: No, you can't, and neither could those doctors. And isn't that a real problem with utilitarianism? I agree that whatever is right will lead to the greatest happiness for the greatest number. The problem is knowing what that is.

Tom: So there is no way of knowing what is right. We can't see into the future; we can't know everything. We've just got to live for today, and I'm happy being gay today, so that's that.

Nick: Is it? Come on, you're a much deeper thinker than that. You don't want to give up that easily. Why not dream with me for a minute. Imagine you could dream of anything. What do we really need in order to find out whether something is right or wrong?

Tom: Someone who could see into the future.

Nick: I agree. Dream with me that there could be someone like that. Someone outside of space and time. Someone who knows everything and can tell us what will bring us the greatest happiness in the long run. Going back to the problem of naturalism, we need someone who can tell us which aspects of our nature are right and which have got screwed up.

Tom: Hang on—I can see where you're going.

Nick: But that's it, isn't it? We're dreaming of God.

Tom: Certainly, if he existed, we wouldn't have any problem knowing what is right and wrong.

Nick: Well, I wouldn't go that far. But we certainly could know what was right if he revealed it to us and we listened to what he said. And even more than that—he might enable us to do it. Because that's yet another problem: I often know what is right, but I just don't want to do it. That's why I need God to enable me to change my mind *and* to give me the power to live it out.

Tom: But that's only if he exists.

Nick: Quite right. The fact that we are dreaming of him doesn't make him exist. But doesn't it make you want to investigate and find out?

Tom was obviously a quick thinker. So it was appropriate to move at the speed I did in that conversation. If the people you are trying to help are not used to thinking in concepts like this, the principles still apply, but you will have to go much more slowly and may find that it takes weeks, months or even years for your friends to discover the inadequacies of the non-Christian worldviews they have absorbed.

I have had conversations along these lines with many students over the years. At the end, not one of them has ever said that he or she wanted to become a Christian right there and then. But that is not the aim of positive deconstruction. All I'm looking for is a heart response that says, "I'm not sure I'm happy with what I believe after all. It might be worth looking at Jesus."

I know that this response has happened many times. I have often found that when I am later speaking at an event, who should come in and stand at the back but that student? When this happens, I get really excited because I see that someone who previously wasn't at all interested in looking at Jesus is now showing some interest.

There is still a long way for such people to go, but at least we are now on the road together. They want to find out something about Jesus. That brings us into the area of proclamation, which we'll look at in part two.

8

We Can Be
Wrong Too

BEFORE WE MOVE INTO PART TWO, we need to stop for a moment and apply the principle of positive deconstruction to ourselves and the things we believe.

I have already indicated that the process of positive deconstruction is relevant not just for non-Christians but also for Christians. We too can be stuck in worldview feedback loops in which we reinforce false beliefs.

The fact that we are Christians does not mean that our worldviews are not also circular. Of course they are. As we saw in chapter two, every worldview is circular. Each worldview tends to reinforce itself. But that doesn't necessarily mean that the worldview is false. A completely true worldview, also, would reinforce itself. What it does mean is that I must recognize that errors in my own worldview will be hard to spot. I have to work hard to discover those of my beliefs that are not actually true but simply self-reinforcing. Then

I will be able to move closer to holding a worldview that is wholly true. Of course, it will still be self-reinforcing, but it will be truth that is being reinforced and not error.

If we are genuinely concerned about truth, we must constantly reassess what we believe. We must try to step outside our feedback loops and ask ourselves some difficult questions. But first of all we must acknowledge the simple but difficult fact that we can be wrong.

As a young Christian I asked a well-respected preacher how I could tell my friends I thought I had found the truth in Jesus, without appearing to be bigoted. "If they think you are bigoted," he said, "that's too bad. But you have to remember that as a Christian you do have the truth, you are right, and you aren't wrong. Don't give an inch on that."

At the time I was just beginning to think about my newfound faith, but there was something about his answer that preyed on my mind. Could I ever claim to have the whole truth? Surely I could be wrong. How could I be infallible? As I grew older in my Christian faith, I began to find out just how often I did get things wrong. I also discovered that this was nothing special about me. As I talked with other Christians and looked at the history of the church I found that all of us easily pick up and maintain false ideas.

Some of my Christian friends are quite convinced that God created the world in six days, a few thousand years ago. Others are equally convinced that God created the world over billions of years, using a gradual process which we can describe with an evolutionary model. They can't both be right. Either one group or the other is wrong. This is just one example of many where we can see that large numbers of Christians must be wrong. Indeed, church history is full of Christians who have gotten it wrong, from Origen's castration[1] to some South African churches' support for apartheid.

Currently a debate is taking place concerning the nature of hell. Some Christians maintain the traditional view of hell as a place of eternal, conscious torment for those who have rejected Christ; others, who hold equally strongly to the Bible as God's revealed Word, suggest that the Bible may really teach that such people will cease to exist (sometimes called "annihilationism" or "conditional immortality").[2] If the latter view turned out to be correct, once again we should have to recognize that the church has been wrong for a very long time!

Clearly, both personal experience and church history teach us that we can be wrong. It is vital, then, that we have a genuine humility as Christians. We must recognize our fallibility and constantly reassess what we believe. If we are committed to truth, and not just to making ourselves comfortable by reinforcing our current worldview, we must be prepared to subject what we believe to a positive deconstruction.

Skepticism Can Be Healthy

For many of us, this will mean rediscovering a healthy skepticism. Skepticism has, historically, taken a variety of forms. But when most Christians use the term, we generally seem to think only of the nihilistic[3] versions which deny all claims to truth (technically called "total negative skepticism") or which refuse to affirm any truth there may be (technically called "Pyrrhonism").[4] There are, however, other, much more positive, forms of skepticism—particularly the one called "skeptical inquiry."[5] This sees skepticism not as a conclusion but as a methodology, a way of seeking after truth. This understanding of skepticism is actually much truer to the original meaning of the word *skeptic*. The Greek word *skeptikos*, from which it is derived, is related to a verb meaning "to consider." We all need to consider what we believe. We are storing up problems for ourselves if we won't.

Working as an evangelist means that I see many people change from being non-Christians to being Christians. Most of the people I have the privilege of leading to Christ were initially very skeptical about everything I presented. Often they were the ones who questioned me very hard in open debates, considering the issues deeply and requiring good evidence before they would accept any belief. As a result, they came to the conclusion that the central message of the gospel is true, and they became Christians. Then many aspects of their lives changed. A lot of these, of course, are very good changes. But unfortunately I have often seen a bad change too. Almost overnight, many, when they become Christians, seem to change from being skeptical to being gullible.

This is due partly to the social pressure that comes with belonging to a new community. They want to fit in with the church or Christian group they have joined. Many seem to say to themselves, "Right, I've believed in Jesus; now what else do I need to believe in as well?" It's as if they attach a giant vacuum cleaner to their brains to suck in all the other beliefs and opinions held by the group. Consequently, they pick up a whole set of ideas covering everything from the consumption of alcohol to the acceptability of rock music, from Sunday shopping to the morality of various fashions.

The tragedy is that, all too often, new Christians like this wake up some time later and realize they can't believe all these ideas any more. And so they give them up. All of them. Including Jesus.

If we truly care about people, wanting to help them not just to come to faith for a while but also to go on and grow as Christians, we must encourage them to think through the ideas they are picking up. And we must do the same with all the ideas we have absorbed since we ourselves became Christians. I suggest that we should all go through the process of positive deconstruction with our own "Christian" beliefs, to assess how far they are truly Christian. And this should be part of our regular, personal, spiritual audit.

The Bible tells us to "test everything" and "hold on to the good" (1 Thess 5:21). Indeed, much of the New Testament was written to early Christians who had adopted all sorts of false teachings and needed to be called back to the true gospel. It is a positive deconstruction of their beliefs.

This is not easy. Neither is it comfortable. It can hurt to let go of beliefs we may have held on to for a long time. Perhaps we have lived with them for so long that they are not just something we believe; they have become a part of us. But as we let go, and as we go through the crisis experience that goes with it, we shall find not only that we get a clearer understanding of truth but also that we develop an appreciation of how non-Christians feel when we ask them to do the same. This will enable us to empathize with them as we help them to subject their beliefs to positive deconstruction.

Let's begin to do that now. Let's ask the three crucial questions about our faith—and see where there is truth about which we can be certain and where there is error that we might discover. Obviously, I can't take all your beliefs and positively deconstruct them, because I don't know what they are. But I can, in the next few pages, give you a little initial help which might guide you as you tackle this for yourself.

Does the Christian Gospel Make Sense?

Some people argue that the Christian gospel cannot make sense because it includes "mystery."

It certainly is true that many aspects of our worldview are mysterious. We believe in God, who is three persons in one; we cannot fully understand this, so we talk about the mystery of the Trinity. We believe that Jesus is both God and human; we cannot fully understand this, so we talk about the mystery of the Incarnation. We believe that the Bible was written down by human beings but is also God's Word to us. As we cannot fully understand this, we talk about the mystery of the inspiration of Scripture.

We are so used to these mysteries that most of us rarely think about them. But others look at our beliefs and challenge their coherence. Some, like atheist Richard Dawkins, would argue that the only good explanation of anything is a scientific one. He has an implicit faith in the all-sufficiency of reductive explanations.[6] Thus he sees a belief in mystery as a cop-out: because we can't give a reductive answer, we give up and call it a mystery. This, he says, will not do. Others, like our Muslim friends, would argue that Islam is far superior to Christian faith because it is more logical and straightforward—without the mysteries.

Certainly, I would agree with Richard Dawkins that the answers the Christian gospel gives to some questions are not reductive. But I wonder why he is so committed to being a reductionist when thinking about the big questions of God and his relationship with us. Isn't it true that, if God really does exist, and created everything there is, and exists outside our space-time framework, then there is no way our minds are ever going to reduce him to a level we can understand? If I could understand everything about him, he would not be much of a God. Isn't it the case that, given the nature of God, a theology that includes mystery actually makes sense? In fact, isn't it the case that any understanding of a Creator-God that does not include mystery cannot make sense? For if God is able to create everything, how could his creatures fully understand him? It seems to me that a belief in a Creator-God requires a belief in the inability of the creatures to understand their Creator fully. That is, if our belief in a Creator-God is to be coherent, it must include some mystery about the nature of God and his relationship with us.

This is illustrated by the argument of our Muslim friends. It is true that Islam does not contain the mystery that is present in the Christian gospel. We wrestle with the mystery of the Trinity, whereas they worship the unitary Allah. We struggle with the mystery of the Incarnation, whereas they teach that Jesus was just a prophet. We try to get our minds round the mystery of inspiration, whereas they believe that the Qur'an was simply dictated by God. We attempt to grasp something of the mystery of substitutionary atonement, whereas they believe in a sort of spiritual accountant who adds up good points and takes away bad points.

If, on looking at those differences, I were asked to decide which of these faiths was revealed by the Creator-God and which was made up by people, it would seem quite clear to me which one was which.

It is true that Islam is more simple and straightforward. But what Muslims see as a strength, I would suggest, is a weakness. Whereas they would say that the simplicity makes their faith more coherent, I would suggest that given the complexity of the subject matter, it actually makes it internally inconsistent.

Given the nature of the God in whom we believe, the core of the Christian gospel does make sense. It is coherent; it does not contain internal inconsistencies. This does not mean that everything that every Christian believes is coherent. We have seen that the core of the gospel is coherent, but what about some other ideas and beliefs which many of us add on? Each of us must look at every belief we hold and ask ourselves whether it makes sense.

Let me give you an example. Some Christians believe very strongly in the "authority of preaching." I have even heard it stated that although one can question and debate things said in normal conversation, anything said from a pulpit is not open for discussion; it must be accepted as from God. (Not surprisingly, this view was proposed from a pulpit, so it could not be questioned.) Setting aside the fact that this is not biblical, it is not even coherent. If I go to different churches, or even the same church at different times, I hear different teaching. At one time I may hear a sermon that contradicts something preached by someone else. I cannot accept it all. It simply does not make sense to say that it all comes from God.

Take another example which struck me recently. I know some Christians who, at different times, have different and contradictory views. Sometimes, when they face problems and obstacles, they say, "These difficulties show that what I wanted to do is not actually God's will. He is closing the door and guiding me away from it." At other times, these same people, when they face problems and obstacles, say, "These difficulties show that I am doing the right thing. The devil is worried and he's trying to put me off." They can't have it both ways. Holding two contradictory beliefs about problems and obstacles does not make sense.

You may be aware of other examples of incoherent beliefs held by Christians. But I am sure you will find that they are all peripheral ideas which have been added on to the core truth of the gospel. The heart of the gospel is entirely coherent, though some of the extra beliefs we add on are not always so. This is a recurrent distinction that we will make as we look at the other two questions.

Does the Christian Gospel Correspond with the Real World?

Many would argue that the claims of the gospel do not correspond with the way the world is.

They might, for instance, say that the claim that Jesus rose from the dead does not correspond with the real world because we know that human beings do not rise from the dead. In particular, they might argue that this is an unscientific view. Science has established the law that people do not rise from the dead; therefore Jesus cannot have done so, and therefore the Christian gospel does not correspond with the way the world is.

That, however, is actually a very unscientific view. By saying that people do not rise from the dead and therefore Jesus could not have done so, they are making what is called an a priori assumption. They have a theory (that human beings do not rise from the dead), and they encounter a claimed observation (that Jesus did rise). Since the claimed observation does not fit with the theory, they say the observation cannot be true. But that is bad philosophy of science. One must always be prepared to reassess one's theories in the light of observations.

Indeed, that is how most of the great advances in science have taken place; when observations have failed to fit with a current theory, the theory has had to be changed. When Galileo observed the phases of Venus, he found they didn't fit with Ptolemy's theory of the sun orbiting the earth—and the theory had to be changed. When Madame Curie was working with pitchblende (an ore containing uranium) and observed a raised radioactivity, this did not fit with the theory that elements cannot transmute into other elements—and the theory had to be changed. Science is all about modifying our theories on the basis of new evidence.

It follows that if the claim that Jesus rose from the dead does not correspond with the theory that people do not rise from the dead, we cannot simply reject it out of hand. We must investigate it and consider what evidence there is for it. If we can't find enough evidence for the resurrection, we can reject it. But if we find that there is enough evidence for it, we must modify the theory. We must recognize that, although human beings do not normally rise from the dead, Jesus did, and that tells us that there was something special about him. We must also take seriously his claim to be no mere human being, but actually God himself come as a human being to die and rise again for us.

It is important to understand that the Christian faith is not based upon an idea or an experience, but upon a historical news event. And that event can be investigated, to see whether there is enough evidence that what we believe happened corresponds with what actually did happen. When we do that, we find good evidence that Jesus did walk on this earth, that he did make the claims that are recorded in the Gospels, that he did die and that he did rise again. That is, we find that the central claims of the Christian gospel correspond to the way the world is.

But once again, the fact that this central core is demonstrably true doesn't mean that every belief every Christian holds corresponds with reality. And once again, each of us must carefully analyze everything we believe, to see if it passes the correspondence test for truth.

Let me give you one example of truth claims that many Christians believed but that did not correspond to reality. Some years ago I attended a large meeting held by a well-known Christian speaker with a nationally recognized healing ministry. Although I had not intended to use it as an opportunity for research, I decided, as the meeting progressed, that I would like to follow up those who, we were told, had been healed. I took careful note of five people whom the speaker definitely pronounced as healed (at which there were great cheers from the audience). After the meeting, I introduced myself to each of these five people and asked if they would mind if I sent them a questionnaire to see how God had healed them. They all willingly agreed. I constructed a simple set of questions which I sent to them about a week later. When I received the questionnaires back, I found that, in fact, not one of the people had been healed. One of them said, "I don't know why God didn't heal me, because he was healing everyone else."

Clearly, the claims this speaker was making, that all these people were being healed, did not correspond with reality. I wrote to the speaker and told him the results of my survey, only to receive a rather curt brushoff.

I have no doubt that God can heal anyone of anything, but we must make sure than any specific claims we make do correspond with reality in this and every other area of our Christian lives. So we must keep asking ourselves this difficult question in order to ensure that the things we believe are actually true.

Does the Christian Gospel Work?

A number of people I have met tell me that they have tried being a Christian in the past, but it didn't work. These people are very hard to help, since they have often had an expectation of how being a Christian should work which doesn't actually correspond to what God promises us.

If the Christian gospel is true, it will work. That is, all that Jesus offers will come true. But this doesn't mean that everything that different Christians believe Jesus offers will come true. Once again, we need to draw a distinction between the core of the gospel and other beliefs that we add on. The Bible makes it clear that if we become Christians, we shall experience many blessings that God has for us—such as peace, joy and a relationship with him. But we also see, throughout the Bible, a difference between the "now" and the "not yet." We are promised a certain amount of peace and joy now, but we don't yet experience the total peace and joy we shall know in heaven. Similarly, our relationship with God is patchy now. There are times when I experience a sense of being so close to God I feel I could reach out and touch him, yet at other times he feels a million miles away. But I know that there will come a time, in heaven, when I shall be in a perfectly intimate relationship with God.

Indeed, the Bible actually promises us many struggles in this world. As Paul says in his letter to the church at Corinth: "I have labored and toiled and have often gone without sleep; I have known hunger and thirst and have often gone without food; I have been cold and naked. Besides everything else, I face daily the pressure of my concern for all the churches" (2 Cor 11:27-28).

If we recognize these struggles and the sense of the "not yet" as well as the "now," we will discover that the Christian gospel does work. As we have seen with the other two questions, however, if we add on extra, unbiblical beliefs, we will find that they do not pass this truth test.

Some Christians, for example, believe that they should expect complete and perfect health in this life. But this is not what the Bible teaches, and those who hope for it will be disappointed. Some believe that God wants us to be wealthy and will give us more money back if we give away what we have. But this approach to giving (as a selfishly motivated investment system) is not biblical and will not deliver. Some believe that if only we pray in a particular way, have a particular experience or learn a particular technique, evangelism will be easy—need I say more?

Communicate the Core

When we subject our faith to a positive deconstruction, then, we find that the core of the gospel is true, but many of the other ideas we develop or adopt may not be.

Among other things, this must teach us that when we are trying to communicate the gospel to other people, it is that core to which we must stick. Of course, we want to think more widely and deeply about other issues for ourselves. We don't want to stay in the middle of our faith; we want to push out to the edges. But when we do so we must recognize that we are likely to get things wrong. So these edges are not the areas into which we should take non-Christians when we are helping them to start thinking about Christian faith. We must help them to find out about the core. I will now develop that in part two, as we look at helping people who want to find out about Jesus.

Part Two

Helping People Who Want to Find Out About Jesus

9

Do I
Understand It?

WHEN I FIRST REALIZED that I needed to find out how to tell
others about Jesus, I began to devour evangelism training manuals.
As a result, I discovered a range of "gospel presentations" that were
clearly laid out for me to use. They sounded great—and so straightforward. Some of them even told me the exact words I should say,
what non-Christians would reply to me, then what I should say back
to them, and so on.

The problem came when I tried to use them. The non-Christians
I spoke to obviously hadn't read the script. They didn't seem to
know what they were supposed to say. Others would listen to me
detailing three simple points or watch me drawing a little diagram,
but it didn't seem to connect with them. I was making a great
presentation, while they seemed to be somewhere else.

Then I looked in the Bible. And I can vividly recall, even now,
the deep shock I experienced. No matter how hard I tried, I couldn't

find any of these simple, universal and complete gospel presentations in the Bible. What I did find was that whenever Jesus talked
with people he used an approach tailored to each individual. The
words he used when talking with the Samaritan woman at the well
were very different from those he used for Nicodemus, and both
were very different from those he used when he encountered the
rich young ruler.

Suddenly it struck me: different people are different. Of
course, it seems obvious now. But somehow I had missed it
before. I had been searching for the one universal gospel presentation, and there is none. God doesn't give us a "gospel
presentation" because there is no one presentation that is appropriate for all people at all times. There is one gospel, but the way
we communicate it will differ according to the types of individuals we are seeking to help. They all have different backgrounds,
experiences, hopes and dreams, hurts and fears. If we are to treat
people as people and not as gospel fodder, we must help different
people in different ways.

I have been a full-time evangelist now for many years, and I
never, ever, use one of the standard gospel presentations from
the evangelism training manuals. They may be helpful for some
people, but I can only say that I never use them. So how do I
explain the gospel to someone who is interested and wants to
find out about Jesus? In this chapter and the next I shall outline
my approach, in the hope that it might be of help to you as you
seek to help others. Essentially I try to start from two points: a
clear understanding of the gospel and a clear understanding of
the person I am trying to help. If I can bring those two together,
I will have succeeded in helping that person to understand the
gospel.

God's gospel is fixed and unchanging, so I can work away on
my own to make sure that I understand it (see the next section). The
person I am trying to help, however, will be different from any other
person I have tried to help, and so I must also try to understand him
and the best way of helping him begin to understand the gospel (see
the next chapter).

What Is the Gospel?

Imagine you have a friend who has become interested in finding out about Jesus. Perhaps she has come to see the inadequacy of the views she previously held, and she now wants to look at this character Jesus Christ. Picture her sitting in an armchair, in your room, with a coffee cup in her hand. Suddenly she says, "You're a Christian, aren't you? Tell me what you believe as a Christian."

You can hardly believe your ears. At last you have an opportunity to explain the Christian gospel to someone. What are you going to say? Where do you start? Do you understand the gospel well enough to be able to help her? Or do you have the same problem I had for many years—you don't really know where to begin? Perhaps you might try to think of all the words you have heard in church. Then you might say them. "It's all about propitiatory atonement," you might tell her. "You see, Christ is the fulfillment of the levitical sacrifices, and salvation is appropriation of the blood."

Of course, all of that is true. But she won't have the faintest idea what you are talking about. In fact, she'll probably assume you must be competing for the Nerd of the Year award (and doing rather well at it). So she'll give up and go down to the pub—and you'll be left talking to the armchair.

Now it may be that you feel God has called you to a specific ministry of evangelizing armchairs. If so, that's the kind of language you need to use, because that way you'll find you have lots of armchairs to talk to! But seriously, if you feel God has called you to reach ordinary people, you will need to use ordinary language. You must use words that can be understood by a generation with little or no Christian heritage. You must employ language that will make sense to a generation for whom the concept of Jesus dying so that we can be forgiven is totally incomprehensible, and for whom the Mount of Olives sounds like a European food surplus.

Is It Really Simple?

At the beginning of this book, when we were looking at Colossians 4, we saw that Paul asked people to pray that he would "proclaim the gospel clearly." The gospel is meant to be proclaimed clearly.

The gospel is simple, not in the sense that it is easy, but in the sense that it doesn't have to be complicated. That doesn't mean that there aren't complicated mysteries in it if we delve more deeply; of course there are. But God, in his goodness to us, has chosen to reveal certain pieces of information in a straightforward way. He has done this so that we can all understand it, whether we are old or young, educated or uneducated.

Now, if God has chosen to reveal the heart of the gospel simply, so that even a young child can respond to it, we must not put obstacles in the way by making it more complicated for them. Having said that, I don't mean that it is going to be easy for us to explain it clearly. If we are to do so, we must understand it clearly ourselves. This means more than just knowing a few key words; it means understanding the underlying concepts.

When I was at school, some teachers' lessons were difficult to understand. Everything they said seemed to be complicated and hard to follow. At the time I thought this was because they were smart and I wasn't. It was only later that I came to see that they made things seem so complicated because they didn't really understand the concepts themselves. If we don't understand something clearly, we'll never be able to explain it clearly.

For many years I didn't understand the gospel well. I had responded to it. (Thankfully, it isn't necessary to understand the gospel fully in order to become a Christian. How much did the thief on the cross understand about substitutionary atonement, I wonder?) But though I had responded, I'd never gone on to think the gospel message through in an orderly way. As a result, I had great difficulty in explaining it simply to other people.

I discovered this inadequacy when Carol and I were leading an open evangelistic youth group at our church. We had up to a hundred teenagers coming each Saturday, and for almost all of them this was their only contact with the church. Through our relationship with them and the way we challenged their thinking, we found that many became interested in hearing about Jesus.

On one particular night, a large group of them asked me to spell out what I believed as a Christian. I made a deal with them. I told them I would try to explain what I believed, but they would have to stop me any time I said anything they didn't understand or that didn't seem to make sense. They were happy to do that, so I set off. We didn't move very fast. I couldn't seem to say a single sentence without confusing them. For a while I wondered if they were just giving me a hard time. But they weren't. They genuinely wanted to know about Jesus. It just seemed that I couldn't explain it clearly. And I realized that this was largely due to the fact that I didn't really understand it clearly myself.

I decided there and then to go home and work hard at it until I did understand the gospel clearly and could explain it simply to people who have no Christian heritage—and therefore no understanding of the fundamental concepts.

In this chapter I want to share with you something of what I learned.

The gospel is not limited to John 3:16, or to any other individual verse for that matter. The problem with isolated verses is that they can be misunderstood if taken out of context. (I heard of a student who said that his favorite verse is the one that says "Woe unto them that rise up early in the morning"—Is 5:11 KJV. What a great verse for students!) No, the gospel is given in the whole Bible, and if we are to understand it properly we must see it in that context. So let's start by trying to get an overall understanding of the whole revelation of God in the Bible. There are many ways of summarizing its content. Here is one I find particularly helpful, to give you an idea of how it might be done.

One Summary of the Bible

Genesis 1 and 2: God set it up. The first two chapters of the Bible tell us that God created this world and created men and women to live in it. He created us to live in a loving relationship with him and with one another.

Genesis 3: We mucked it up. Adam and Eve chose to reject God. And we have all continued this by rejecting God ourselves. God came looking for Adam in the garden but couldn't find him; the relationship with God had been broken. Adam and Eve used fig leaves to cover themselves, because they wanted to hide from each other; their relationship with each other had been broken.

Genesis 4 to Malachi: God called us back. Lots of events are recounted in the Old Testament, and many themes run through it. But at its heart it is the story of God calling men and women back to himself and to one another. God still loves us and wants us to come back into a proper relationship with himself and with other people.

Matthew to John: God came himself. Unfortunately, men and women kept rejecting God. So God came himself, in the person of his Son Jesus. He came to call us back into a proper relationship with himself and to provide a way for us to respond, by dying for us on the cross. His death wasn't an accident; he intended to die, and, in so doing, to take the death penalty we deserve for everything wrong we have ever done. We can now be forgiven and return to a proper relationship with God and with one another.

Acts to Jude: God grows relationships. God wants us to grow in our relationship with him and with one another. So he shows us how that can happen. On earth this relationship is growing but is still only partial. When we die, we shall enter into a perfect relationship with God and with one another. The Bible calls it "heaven."

Revelation: God is going to sort it out. If we won't come back to God and receive the forgiveness he offers, the Bible emphasizes that our relationship with God and with other people will become increasingly broken. Ultimately, we shall face a total separation from God and from one another. The Bible calls it "hell."

Of course, there is far more to the Bible than is given in my brief summary. We could spend years studying it and never fully understand all that is in it for us. Indeed, the more I know about the Bible, the more I realize how much I don't know, and the more I want to study what it says. But there is a danger in delving more and more deeply into the Bible. We can lose our grip on the basic, simple gospel message. That's why it is very important, whatever the depth of our understanding of the Bible, to have this simple gospel message sorted out in our minds. To help with that, let's put some even simpler headings next to those I gave in the summary above.

Genesis 1 and 2: God set it up	God
Genesis 3: We mucked it up	Us
Genesis 4 to Malachi: God called us back }	God
Matthew to John: God came himself	
Acts to Jude: God grows relationships	What if I do?
Revelation: God is going to sort it out	What if I don't?

This gives us a very simple summary,[1] as follows.

God. There is a God who created us. He designed us to live in an intimate personal relationship with him and with one another. We are created for love, to love God and to love one another.

Us. Men and women don't want to live in a relationship with God, so we've turned our backs on him and decided to go our own way, to do our own thing. As a result we have each lost our relationship with God and with one another.

God. God still loves us and wants us to live in a proper relationship with himself and with one another. That's why he came to earth in the person of Jesus—to call us back into those proper relationships and to provide the way for us to do so. As he died on the cross, he took the death penalty we deserve for everything wrong we've ever done, so that we can be forgiven, and so that relationships can be restored.

What if I do? If I say that I'm sorry and that I do want to turn around and live in a proper relationship with God and with others, God will restore me to those relationships. These relationships are patchy here on earth, but they grow, and when I die I will live in a perfect relationship with God and with others. That's heaven.

What if I don't? If I refuse to turn back to God, there is nothing more he can do for me. God did all he could for me when Jesus came and died for me. If I choose to reject him, I am consigning myself to separation from him and from other people—an increasing separation on earth and then, when I die, a total separation. That's hell.

This Is for You, Not for Them

Let me stress that what I have laid out here is not a "gospel presentation." It isn't a scheme for presenting the message of Jesus to other people. It is simply a tool for understanding the gospel ourselves, so that we will be better equipped to explain it simply to others.

If people ask you what you believe as a Christian, I am not suggesting that you reply, "God, us, God, what if I do? what if I don't?"—and give them the whole thing in one shot. There is no way that they will be able to take in one of these points all at once, let alone all of them. It usually takes time, a lot of time, and many questions and answers, for people to understand any part of the gospel.

If you use this structure as a way of getting the gospel straight in your mind, however, when people ask you what you believe, you will be sure about what you are trying to communicate.That way, if you are not using your brain power to try to remember the gospel, you can use it, instead, to pray for wisdom and to focus on the people to whom you are talking. Thus you will be able to help them in the way most appropriate to them at the time. Let's look at that in the next chapter.

10

Can I
Explain It?

I HAD JUST FINISHED AN EVENT in a college. People were milling about and talking; music was playing; noise was everywhere. A student came straight over to me and asked, through the hubbub, if we could talk.

"Of course," I replied.

"I've got a problem," she began. She took a deep breath, gritted her teeth, and said (well, I thought she said—I was convinced she said), "I've just found out I can't eat chocolate."

"Oh dear," I replied lightly, trying to brighten the atmosphere. "Are you allergic?"

At that point she burst into tears.

"Wait a minute," I said. "Sit down here and tell me again what you said, will you?"

She lowered herself onto a chair, wiped her eyes with her hand, took a deep breath and said, more slowly and audibly this time,

"I've just found out I can't have children."

My heart stopped, my jaw dropped and I started praying for the Second Coming right there and then. How could I have been so insensitive? Why hadn't I heard what she had said?

Thankfully she understood the effect of all the noise around, and I was able to help her and pray with her. But I realized again that day, if I didn't know it before, how important it is to listen carefully to what other people say.

Christians have often been criticized for giving the answer before we know what the question is. That is a valid criticism. And it must be so annoying for people who have to suffer us. Have you ever listened to a politician being interviewed and realized that he has a particular message he wants to give, and he is going to get it in, whatever the interviewer asks? And have you felt annoyed and frustrated listening to it? Now imagine how people feel when we try to tell them what we want to tell them, regardless of what questions they are asking or where they are in their lives.

If we are truly to help people when they ask us about Jesus, we must communicate aspects of the gospel that are relevant to them where they are, not just launch into some presentation we have learned. This will mean listening to them carefully and not just talking at them. It might mean asking them a few questions, if that is appropriate. We might raise a question such as whether they have thought much about Jesus in the past; whether they have been to church and, if they have, what they thought about it; why they are now interested in finding out about Jesus.

Meanwhile, as we listen to them, we must also listen to God. When I talk with people I pray that, in addition to whatever natural wisdom I may have, God will give me a supernatural insight into how best I can help them.

Of course, if my mind is on both the person I am trying to help and God, I can't also concentrate on remembering the gospel. I can just about do two things at once, but not three. So you can see why it is so important to have a clear understanding of the gospel in your mind so that it becomes second nature and you don't even have to think about it. Only then will you be able to concentrate on the other person and on God. (At this point you might want to go back and read the last chapter again.) As God gives me a special insight, or as I am able to work it out through talking with the person, I am thus in a position to try to communicate whichever aspect of the gospel is most relevant to that individual.

But how do I communicate that aspect of the gospel? In years gone by, one would have just told it straight as a set of propositions. That is the way many of us have been taught to communicate the gospel. And that was appropriate for people who were brought up in a culture of modernism. As we saw in chapter two, however, our culture is now rapidly moving into postmodernism, and there is a deep suspicion or outright rejection of propositions. Postmodernism has replaced propositional truth with stories. A classic example of this is Douglas Coupland's postmodern book *Generation X,* which doesn't provide a set of propositions detailing the culture he sets out to describe, but tells a series of stories about people who, themselves, spend their time telling stories.

Storytelling

This aspect of postmodernism presents us with a challenge and an opportunity. The challenge is to communicate God's constant gospel to a new and different culture. The opportunity stems from the fact that, as well as containing series of propositional truths (such as those found in Paul's letter to the Romans), the Bible also contains many stories (from Old Testament battles to New Testament parables). Such is the breadth of Scripture, given for all people in all times, that there are sections particularly relevant for each culture.

Throughout modernism, it was often appropriate for us to use sequences of propositions from the Bible to communicate the gospel (the so-called Roman Road, for instance, which presented the gospel through a series of statements in Romans). As we move into postmodernism, the Bible is just as relevant as it always was, and it always will be. But in our evangelism we shall very often do better at first to emphasize the stories.

Missiologists tell us that different parts of the Bible are always initially more useful for some cultures than others. Indeed, parts of the Bible seem to have been written with that in mind. For instance, Matthew seems to have been written for a Jewish readership, while Luke was apparently written for the Greeks. Similarly, one wouldn't start with Mark's Gospel in evangelism with Muslims, because it begins by referring to Jesus as the Son of God and would therefore raise instant objections.

Now, as we think about our culture missiologically, we can see that the New Testament letters may have been useful for the age of modernism, but as we move into postmodernism we would be better advised to make more use of the stories. Of course, that doesn't mean that we abandon the rest of Scripture. Far from it! It is all inspired by God and profitable (2 Tim 3:16). We must, however, be wise in the way we introduce people to the Scriptures.

Let me give you some examples showing how we might communicate aspects of the gospel that are most relevant to particular people, using Bible stories to do that. Imagine that someone has asked me what I believe as a Christian and, if appropriate, I have chatted with him a bit to find out where he is coming from. I might then begin to open up the gospel for him, starting at one of the five points we saw in the last chapter, and using relevant stories.

God

I might begin at the first point, using stories to help the inquirer to discover that God created us so that we could enjoy a loving relationship with him and with other people.

Perhaps I might invite him to look with me at Mark 12:28-34. This is a story in which Jesus is put on the spot as someone asks him which is the greatest commandment. It's like asking what is the most important thing in life. How is Jesus going to answer? You can almost feel the tension in the air. "Love," he says, as he quotes the Old Testament commands to love God and your neighbor.

In my experience these words of Jesus strike a deep chord in the hearts of many people. Students, particularly, know that love is important. If they fall in love with a new boyfriend or girlfriend, suddenly nothing else matters. "Lectures? Forget them. I'm in love, man."

If you start in this way, you might find that the conversation develops into a consideration of the love that we hear about in this world and the love that Jesus talked about. Certainly most students' idea of love is romantic love—that strange feeling you have in the pit of your stomach, as if you are about to throw up. But Jesus talks about and shows love of another kind, which sacrifices all for those who don't deserve it. Again, there are some great stories here—such as the love of the father who runs to his prodigal son to welcome him back, and the love of Jesus who sets out to Jerusalem to die for us.

Of the many ways in which the conversation may develop, a number may be of real interest to the person with whom you are talking, and all will enable you to use biblical stories to communicate something of the gospel of Jesus Christ, who loves us and wants us to live in a loving relationship with him and others.

As I have already said, this is not a universal answer. There will be those for whom love is a difficult concept. They may never have known the love of a parent, or of anyone else for that matter. They may be confused, negative or cynical about love.

Some years ago, Carol and I met a young homeless girl with serious emotional problems. She came to live with us for a while. One night she started to tell us about her boyfriend, who had said that he loved her. Suddenly she paused and looked puzzled. "I think I love him," she said. "I don't know. I just don't seem to know what love is."

I cried.

It may not help people like this if we begin by telling them that God has created us to enjoy relationships with him and with everyone. Although it is perfectly true, and they will need to understand it at some point, this may simply not be the best place for them to begin. It may be better to start on the second point, which we shall look at now.

Us

Perhaps the person I am talking with has been badly hurt by terrible things that have happened to him. He may have seen his world falling apart, or he may have never known a world that was together at all. I might start trying to help this person by using stories to help him discover that although this world is in a mess, this is not how God wants it to be; the world has gotten mucked up.

For instance, I might invite him to look with me at Luke 4:14-21. This is another great story, full of dramatic tension as Jesus takes the scroll and reads of God's promise to bring good news to the poor and to release the oppressed. Then he says, "Today this scripture is fulfilled in your hearing." This world is not how God intended it to be, or how he wants it to be. It has become mucked up because we can't live in his world in his way, and something must be done about it.

If appropriate, I might invite the inquirer to look with me at one of the many occasions when Jesus showed that he was on the side of the outsider. Depending upon the person, I might invite him to look with me at how Jesus took the side of the moral outsider (the woman caught in adultery, Jn 8), the social outsider (the Samaritan woman at the well, Jn 4), and the superstitious outsider (the leper, Mt 8). Wherever I look, I shall be trying to use the story to help him discover that this world is not how God originally intended it to be; it has become mucked up because we have all turned our backs on him.

Alternatively, it may be that the person I am seeking to help is aware that the problem is not just "out there," but also within himself. He might realize that he keeps mucking things up and causing problems in his own life and for those around him. He might want to change but feel powerless to do anything about it. He might feel out of control. If this is the case, I might begin with a part of my personal story. One of the reasons I wanted to become a Christian was that I kept hurting people, and I couldn't seem to change; then I saw how God could change someone like me.

I might invite the inquirer to look with me at Mark 2:21-22, where Jesus tells some short stories about sewing patches onto garments and putting wine in wineskins. What I want to help him discover is that Jesus offers us an opportunity for a complete new start and a new nature. The gospel shows that we are not stuck with our old habits and weaknesses; we can be changed. That may be just what this inquirer needs to discover.

Again, it may be that the people who have hurt this person in the past have claimed to be Christians. I meet many people like that, and they are negative and cynical not only about love in general but also about Jesus in particular. Asking them what they think of Christians is a bit like asking a lamp post what it thinks of dogs. How do we help someone who was forced to sit through hours of boring chapel at school, or pressurized into agreeing with beliefs he didn't share and was never allowed to question, or (worse still) sexually abused by a Christian?

I usually find, in this situation, that the first step is to help him separate the historical Jesus from the Christians of his experience. To do this I might invite him to look with me at Matthew 7:15-23, where Jesus tells some stories about fruit trees and about people who come to him boasting of all the fine religious things they have done. Jesus tells them dramatically, "I never knew you." I want to help this person to discover that not everyone who claims to be a Christian really is. It is a tragedy if we reject Jesus because of what some people profess to be doing in his name.

Whenever I focus on this area, my aim is to help the person discover that his experience of pain and suffering (his own story) is actually what the gospel predicts (the gospel story) in a world which has turned its back on God.

It can be very helpful to some people to talk with them about the suffering they have experienced. Others, however, don't want to dwell on the problem; they want solutions. In that case, I might not begin at this point of the gospel at all, but rather at the next.

God

Whenever appropriate, it is great to start right at the central point of the gospel: the person and work of Jesus. I want to tell people the story of Jesus.

Incidentally, I find it really hard to say the word *Jesus,* and many others have told me they have the same problem. I don't know why this is—whether it's just a psychological block or something spiritual. For some reason, it always seems so much easier to talk about "church" or "my faith" or "my belief." It's even easier to talk about "Christianity" than about Jesus. But the center of the gospel is Jesus, and we must talk about him rather than about our faith in him. I've had the privilege of taking some part in the training of a few new evangelists, and I try to get them to forget the word *Christianity* and never to use it. We are not talking about Christianity, or our faith, or church. We are talking about Jesus: his life, his teaching, his claims, his death, his resurrection and his call for us to follow him. So, if it is appropriate, I might begin with some of the great claims of Jesus. These are not cold, hard propositions; they are given within the context of the story of Jesus with us, and many of them are themselves little picture stories.

Jesus said that he came to do many things: to fulfill the law and the prophets (Mt 5:17); to give his life as a ransom (Mt 20:28); to bring fire on the earth (Lk 12:49); to seek and save the lost (Lk 19:10); to give us a full life (Jn 10:10); and to save the world (Jn 12:47). Each one of these will strike a chord with different people at different times, and I might use one or more of them as appropriate.

Ultimately, of course, Jesus came to die. The crucifixion didn't come as a surprise to Jesus, nor was it some dreadful mistake. Jesus was quite sure that he had come to die, and he regularly predicted his own death. At a suitable point, I must help individuals to understand that Jesus came to die for them, to take the death penalty they deserve for everything wrong they have done, so that they can be forgiven and come back into a proper relationship with God and other people.

I must help people to understand this only at a suitable point, because it is rarely appropriate to begin at that part of the story. That is our goal, not usually our starting point. It is the central fact of the gospel, but it isn't easy for people to accept or even to understand this truth. Paul said that the cross is "foolishness to those who are perishing" (1 Cor 1:18), and you don't have to work in evangelism for long to see that fact demonstrated. In many missions, I have found that an audience that was listening attentively will become restive when I begin to speak about the cross. People will even walk out and make it obvious that they don't want to hear about it.

That is why, in most missions, I won't even mention the story of the cross, and certainly not attempt to teach about it, until several days into the week. And when I am talking with individuals about Jesus, I am cautious about bringing them to the cross lest I should do it too early and put a stumbling block in their way. Bringing them to the cross is my goal, but I must be careful not to try to get there too early.

It might be appropriate, however, for me to start by talking about Jesus in the ways suggested above. Conversely, it might be better, with a particular inquirer, to begin by talking about myself and what it means for me to be a Christian—and thus about what is available to him too, if he comes to faith in Christ.

What If I Do?

Having said this, we must be careful with testimony, because testimony is not the gospel. The gospel is all about Jesus: who he is, what he has done and what he is continuing to do. Our testimony will illustrate the gospel and explain how Jesus is acting in our lives, but it is not the gospel. Furthermore, I need to be sure that the other person wants to hear my story, and that it is not just that I want to talk about *me*. We all like to talk about ourselves, and there are few things more boring than having to listen to some conceited person who wants you only as an audience while he talks about himself. We are not to be like that, but we do need to be prepared to tell people what it means for us to live in a relationship with God.

I don't know about you, but I find that my relationship with God is patchy. As I said in chapter eight, there are times when I feel so close to God that I could reach out and touch him. Sometimes I have been very aware of God with me, speaking to me, guiding me, pointing out my sin and lovingly forgiving and changing me. But there are other times when I feel as if God must be a million miles away, if he exists at all.

When I tell someone what it means to be a Christian, I try to be as honest about that as I can. Ultimately, we shall have a perfect relationship with God and with one another, but in this life we experience one that comes and goes.

In particular, I make sure that I am honest about the cost of being a Christian. It isn't easy following Jesus. You find yourself swimming against the tide for the rest of your life. We don't want to hide this from people, and, as we shall see in part four, we normally don't want people to become Christians without counting the cost. Once again, however, this is a destination and not a departure point. If we want to help people to develop their interest in Jesus, it might be a mistake to stress the cost too early.

What If I Don't?
I'm not going to spend very long on the "what if I don't?" part of the gospel, because I don't think it is a good place to start.

If you want, you could begin by telling people, "I believe that if you're not a Christian you're going to burn in hell." It may be true, but perhaps it isn't the best way to help people to want to find out more about Jesus. That doesn't mean that we mustn't talk about hell and judgment—far from it. But I find that it's best to let others raise it (they usually will, eventually), rather than raising it myself. And I have never yet begun at this point.

Just the Beginning
We have seen that there are many ways to begin telling people about Jesus. Once you have begun, there are many ways in which the conversation could develop. There is no one universal gospel presentation. There is one gospel, but there are many different ways of explaining it to the many different people in this world. Once you have begun to tell people about Jesus, however, you find that you *are* just beginning.

Whatever way you begin to explain the gospel, people will soon come back with questions. Sometimes these will be questions of clarification as they ask you to explain more about this message of Jesus. But often they will be objections and criticisms. In part three we shall look at how we can answer those questions and "give the reason for the hope" that we have (1 Pet 3:15).

Part Three

Part Three

Helping People with Difficult Questions

11

Giving the Reason for the Hope

A LOT OF MY TIME IS SPENT inviting people to ask me any questions or make any objections they want. These open debates are a major part of my ministry. In fact, someone said recently that I am known for my "debatable qualities." I'm not sure what he meant by that.

Regularly I tell groups of students what I believe as a Christian, and then say, "Most of you won't have agreed with much of what I have said. You will have questions and criticisms. Would you like to fire away with them now?" After that almost anything can happen. It's very scary. I never know what questions will come up or where the debate is likely to go.

You may not be faced with questions from large groups of people, but you can be sure that whenever you are talking with non-Christians, they will eventually start asking you difficult questions about your faith. How are you going to handle these questions?

In this part of the book I want to try to give you some guidelines. As examples, we'll look at three of the most common questions. Obviously, these three will not be the only questions you will ever be asked. This isn't meant to be an exhaustive consideration of all the issues people raise, but I hope the selection will serve to illustrate the principles and increase your confidence in dealing with them.

What Is Apologetics?

This area of evangelism is sometimes called "apologetics." This has nothing to do with apologizing; we are not being apologetic about our faith. Rather, the word comes from the Greek *apologia*, meaning "a reasoned defense." It is not a specifically Christian word, and it could be applied to any belief. One could be an apologist (someone who engages in apologetics) for animal rights, or the free market, or the Labor Party. But, of course, in this book we shall look at what it means to give a reasoned defense for the Christian faith.

Whatever questions we face, we must bear in mind certain guiding principles as we help people find answers.

1. Tell the truth. Truth must be fundamentally important to us as Christians. Jesus claimed to be the truth, and he said that the devil is the father of all lies. If that is the case, there is nothing less godly than telling a lie, and we must make sure that we tell the truth at all times.

That may seem obvious, but when you are under pressure, facing difficult questions, it is tempting to exaggerate or bend the truth to make your case seem stronger. I have seen it happen, and you probably have too.

How many times have you heard Christians exaggerate their testimony? I once heard the lead singer of a Christian band say: "Before I became a Christian, life was terrible, but now it's great. I never have any problems—I'm happy all the time." If that was true, it would be great, but it simply isn't true for him or for any other Christian this side of heaven.

It's not just people's testimonies that get exaggerated, but also facts and evidence. Some Christians will tell you, quite confidently, that there is far more evidence for the existence of Jesus than for the existence of Julius Caesar. I don't know where they get that from. It sounds impressive, but I don't think it's true. They might tell you that there are a great many historical references to Jesus. Again, that sounds impressive, but it isn't true. There are some references to Jesus in histories other than the Bible, but it is not true to say that there are a great number of them.

If we truly follow Christ, we must tell the truth, even if it seems to weaken our case.

2. Recognize the mysteries. Some years ago I was speaking at a mission at a college in Winchester. I opened the major "Grill a Christian" debate (as it was called) to questions from the floor, and was surprised to find that the first few questions were all ones to which there are no clear answers.

The first was, "Where exactly is heaven?"

What did he want—a grid reference? I told him as much as I could, but basically I had to say, "I don't know."

The next question was similar: "What exactly is heaven like? Describe it to me."

Again, I told her as much as I could, but essentially I had to say, "I don't know."

The next few questions followed in the same way. Then a bright spark in the front called out, "You don't seem to know much, do you?" And they all broke out laughing.

But that was the turning point of the debate. They realized I wasn't a slick salesman with a set, watertight presentation. They saw that I was a real person, and that I too was struggling with questions, mysteries and uncertainties. In short, they realized that I was one of them, and that I was on their side.

In the same way, each of us must acknowledge that there are many questions we cannot answer. Sometimes that is because we ourselves don't know the answer, and sometimes it is because no one knows the answer: it is a mystery.

But There Are Answers Too

That doesn't mean that there are no clear answers to any questions.

Far from it. After this Winchester debate, I had tea with the principal of the college and told him what had happened. "That's why I like having you at my college, Nick," he replied. "You recognize that religion is all about mysteries."

I swallowed hard. "Actually, I disagree. It seems to me that the gospel of Jesus is a mixture of mysteries and certainties."

There are great mysteries, but there are also things about which we can be certain. Deuteronomy 29:29 puts it this way: "The secret things belong to the LORD our God, but the things revealed belong to us and to our children for ever, that we may follow all the words of this law." That is, there are "secret things," mysteries known only to God. They are too complex for our brains even to begin to work out, and we shall never understand them. But there are also things that God has revealed to us. Why? So that "we may follow all the words of this law." In New Testament language, that means, "so that we may come to know God through Christ." There are huge mysteries, then, but also great certainties.

There aren't many spiritual things about which I am certain. In fact, I can number them on the fingers of one hand, but they are the things that really matter. I am certain that God is there. I am certain that he loves us. I am certain that Jesus is God become human—and that he came to call us back into a relationship with him and to die so that we could be forgiven. I am certain that because of what Jesus has done for me, I shall go to be with him eternally. I am certain that Jesus will come again.

Outside of those great certainties there are huge mysteries. Where exactly heaven is and what exactly heaven is like are just two of the many questions to which we cannot have complete answers.

God has not revealed everything we want to know. But he has revealed everything we need to know so that we can become and live as Christians. And I am not going to let what I cannot understand stop me from receiving what I can understand.

When you answer questions, then, do express your certainty about the certainties, but also remember to articulate your uncertainty about the mysteries. Liberals make a great mistake when they try to turn every question into an uncertain mystery. But evangelicals can make just as big a mistake by trying to turn every question into a dogmatic certainty.

3. Look for the question behind the question. Most of the people you are trying to help will not have had the time or the opportunity to think through the questions they are asking. So the question they express may not actually be the question they want answered. I find that it helps to reflect the question back to them by saying something like "Sorry, I'm not sure if I've understood you. Are you saying . . . ?" Then they have a chance to sort out their thoughts and perhaps restate the question. It's very frustrating for people if they try to ask a question and you answer a different one. As we saw earlier, this means that we must listen carefully to what they say and not jump in with an answer.

Too Much Truth!
A story is told of a little boy who asked his father, "Where did I come from?"

The father took a deep breath, sat his son down and gave him a long detailed explanation of sexual reproduction. When he eventually finished, he asked his son if that helped him.

"No," said the boy, looking very puzzled. "John says he comes from Birmingham. Where did I come from?"

Sometimes we must ask people to clarify the question before we set about attempting to answer it. Sometimes, also, it can be helpful to find out *why* someone is asking that particular question. For instance, take someone who asks why God allows suffering. It may be a purely academic question—or it may be that her mother has just died. The approach and sensitivity required will be different, depending upon the situation.

4. Don't force people to agree with you. As well as asking people whether or not I have understood their question, I also find it helpful to ask whether they have understood the answer. But as I do so, I try to make sure that I don't seem to be forcing them into a situation where they have to agree with me (or pretend to do so).

There is a big difference between understanding my answer and agreeing with it. People may totally disagree with what I have said, but I need to make sure that they have understood what I meant. So I often say things like, "Is that OK?" I don't mean, "Do you agree with me?" but "Have I expressed myself clearly?" That leaves them free to reply (as they often do): "I understand your answer; I just don't agree with it."

It's their privilege to disagree with me, but I consider it to be my fault if they misunderstand me.

5. *Don't try to prove yourself at other people's expense.* When engaging in debate, we may be in danger of wanting to prove how clever we are. But we do so at our listeners' expense. It is vital to remember that we are there to serve them and not to use them to bolster our ego. One of the greatest compliments I've received in my ministry came in the middle of a large open debate, when a student said, "This isn't at all like I thought it would be. I thought there would be a big wall, with you on one side and us on the other, and we would be lobbing bombs at each other. But it's not like that. You've come around to our side of the wall and you're helping us to climb over." I am so glad that this student recognized that I was on their side. I try to make sure that others realize that too.

I find that open debates, and many individual conversations, go through two clear phases. At first, non-Christians often seem to want to fight. In this initial stage, they ask their questions aggressively. They want to knock me down. They want to make me look stupid. In short, they seem to see me as the enemy. That's understandable, since they might, in the past, have been worked over by apparently unthinking dogmatic Christians, and they assume that I am like that. "Give me ten minutes with him," I've overheard people say, "and I'll show that what he says is a load of rubbish." They don't seem interested in listening to my answers or engaging with me in thinking about the issues.

As this first phase progresses, however, they discover that no matter how they treat me, I am not aggressively antagonistic in return. Neither am I dogmatic. As they begin to see this, their attitude changes. Now we move into phase two. They realize that we are on the same side, and their responses change from being accusatory ("There's no evidence that Jesus ever existed") to interrogative ("What evidence is there that Jesus existed?").

Once a debate moves into this second phase, it can run and run. I've known open debates to go on for hours. The longest I ever took part in ran for four and three-quarters hours. At the end of that, those who were non-Christians still wanted to keep going. I couldn't. My brain had turned to scrambled eggs. But that was a significant time, and a good number of students became Christians through it—even some who had asked the most antagonistic questions.

6. Be aware that your answer will influence the next question. We are not to manipulate people; we are to serve them. If they have genuine questions about a particular area of Christian faith, then we must answer them. It is not right to divert them from it because we want to talk about something else.

Having said that, we often have to face the fact that our conversation will be short, and we want to make the most of the opportunity. If I have only a few minutes with people who are at this stage, as much as possible I want to be answering questions about Jesus and not peripheral issues. I can't manipulate the conversation or say, "I don't want to answer that question, but let me tell you about Jesus!" When they have asked me one question, however, I often have a choice of ways in which I can answer it, and I want to answer in such a way that their next question is about Jesus. This is possible, because the answer I give to one question will have a major influence upon the next question.

Directing the Flow

Suppose someone asks, "How do you know that God exists?" There are many ways I can begin to answer this. Each one will tend to trigger a different set of subsequent questions. If we have a lot of time, it won't really matter what these subsequent questions are. But if we have only a few minutes to talk, I want to answer in such a way that the most likely subsequent questions are about Jesus. Let's look at the answers I might give.

I might point out how the world around, with its apparently designed complexity, appears to indicate an intelligent creator who put it all together. They are then most likely to respond with a set of questions and objections about evolution, like "Hasn't Darwin shown how the world could have come about without God?" Those are interesting questions which can be helpful for people to consider. And if we have plenty of time, it is good to answer lots of questions about this. If I have only a few minutes with someone, however, I would rather be answering questions about Jesus.

I might instead suggest that the beautiful world around points to an amazing artist behind it all. But they will probably come back with a set of questions and objections about the ugliness, pain and suffering in the world. Again, these are important questions that we need to help people to think through. But if I have only a few minutes with someone, I would rather we were talking about Jesus.

Another way of proceeding would be to talk about my experience of God. But they might then respond with questions and objections about whether my faith is simply a psychological delusion, or about people who follow other religions and claim to have had experiences of God. These also are important questions that we need to help people with. But if I have only a few minutes with someone, I would rather be discussing Jesus.

So I would probably tell the story of Jesus' claim to be God become human. If this is true, if Jesus really is God, we know that God exists. Here he is, come to show us that he really is there. The person will then be likely to come back with questions and objections such as, "Did Jesus really claim to be God?" or "How did he prove his claim?" These subsequent questions are all centered around Jesus.

This approach is not manipulating people; it is choosing a valid option that leads them toward questions about Jesus rather than away from them.

7. *Use lots of stories and illustrations.* We looked at this principle of storytelling in chapter ten. If we are to answer the questions of people growing up in this postmodern culture, we must give not just a set of propositions but also lots of illustrations. I have sometimes been most helpful to a questioner when I haven't used a proposition at all in answering the question but simply said, "Let me give you an illustration . . ." and then allowed the story to speak for itself.

A young woman, for instance, once objected to the gospel by saying that it was too restrictive. "How," she asked, "could you expect me to believe that God is loving if he is going to restrict me?"

I replied by telling her a story. "My little boy has started to crawl," I said, "and he is into everything. He particularly likes the fire and could get badly burned. So I have put up a fireplace screen. It restricts him from burning himself and sets him free to go wherever he wants without getting hurt. I have put that restriction there because I love him."

The story didn't need an explanation. Her face showed that she had understood.

8. Remember that you are not alone. Blind terror used to grip me when I first started inviting groups of people to ask me any question they liked. I had no idea what they were going to ask. How could I ever be prepared to answer them?

You, no doubt, feel the same when people ask you difficult questions about your faith. There is no way that any of us can carry all the information we need in order to answer every single question we might be asked. So what can we do?

Listen to the Spirit

First of all, we can realize we are not alone. God is with us, living inside us by his Holy Spirit. We cannot know how to answer every question. But God, through his Spirit, can enable us to know what we need to know in order to answer the questions we are going to face today.

This became evident to me some years ago, when I was speaking at a college mission near Southampton. As I always do, I spent some time in the morning before the main open debate praying that God would show me what I should study so that it would be clear in my mind for the debate. I then experienced one of those (to me, rather rare) occasions when God seemed to speak to me precisely and specifically. I sensed God telling me to study the use of the word *Lord* in the New Testament.

By then, I had conducted quite a number of missions and had been in scores of open debates. Through them all, this particular issue had never come up (nor has it done so in the countless debates and conversations I have had since). I was puzzled, but knew I must obey God, who had spoken so definitely to me. I took various textbooks from my shelves and looked up the subject. It was interesting to find that the Greek word for *Lord,* used as a form of address, just means "Sir" or "Master." But the main way it is used in the New Testament is rather different. There, it usually equates to the Old Testament name for God, Yahweh, which appears in our English versions as "the LORD." So when people referred to Jesus as *Lord,* they were as good as saying that he was God.

This was all very fascinating. But I honestly thought it was about as relevant to evangelism as a knowledge of seventeenth-century church architecture. Still, I had obeyed God.

I entered the gym, where the debate was to be held, and it soon filled with students. I gave a short introductory talk and threw the session open for questions. The first one came immediately, from a student who told me he was studying theology. He was scathingly dismissive of all I had said. He spoke well and roused the audience against me. He concluded by saying, "How can you believe that Jesus was really God? When they called him 'Lord,' it just meant 'Sir' or 'Master.' " For a few seconds I was open-mouthed—not because of his question, but because of the way God had prepared me for it.

In the same way, you are not alone. I don't believe that God will give you knowledge by some sort of magical process. But, if you ask him and are prepared to serve him, he will lead you (sometimes in remarkable ways) to study what you need to know in order to answer the questions you will face today.

I don't know what those questions will be, and neither do you. But there are certain ones that seem to come up time and time again, so in the rest of this part of the book I shall offer some help with three of them. Of course, by now you won't expect me to give you pat answers, for there are none. But I will try to give lots of bits of information and illustrations from which you might like to draw as appropriate when you are answering these questions.

12

If God Is So Good, Why Is the World So Bad?

I CAN'T TELL YOU HOW MANY hundreds of open debates I have carried out in which students and others have been invited to ask me any question they wish. But I can tell you that, in almost every one, someone will ask about suffering. So if you are serious about evangelism, you will need to make sure you can help people with this very big question. As I said before, I am not going to give you pat answers, but to suggest some ideas, illustrations and information which I hope will go some way to helping you as you try to respond to this question.

An Explanation or a Solution?
It is important to help people see the distinction between an *explanation* of suffering and a *solution* for it. As we shall see in a minute, God doesn't provide a complete explanation of suffering, but he does provide a complete solution for it.

Imagine that you are out walking and you get run over by a bus. You lie on the ground in agony as I approach and kneel down at your side. "Let me give you an explanation of your suffering," I say. "You see, the bus has driven over your femur, breaking it in two places. The displaced bone is pressing against your femoral nerve, which is sending neural messages through your lumbar plexus, up your spine and into the pain receptors in your brain, giving you the experience of excruciating agony."

Does that help? Of course not. But suppose instead I say, "I haven't got a complete explanation of your suffering, but I have got a solution for it. I have an injection of morphine here which will take away your pain. I can then splint your leg and take you to a hospital to get it fixed."

Which of these would you prefer? Wouldn't you much rather have the solution than the explanation?

The good news of Jesus is that he provides us with a complete solution to our suffering. The tragedy is, however, that many people will not accept that solution unless they can also have a definitive explanation of our suffering. We can't. My appeal to people is not to put off accepting God's solution until they have a full explanation—because they never will.

In the second half of this chapter we shall look at God's solution for suffering. But let's first see how much of an explanation God does provide. Although it isn't complete, we shall see that it is by no means empty, and, in fact, it is the best one around.

An Incomplete Explanation

Every religion tries to provide some kind of explanation of why God allows suffering. And they are all inadequate. Muslims believe that suffering is due to God. Anything that happens is the will of Allah. If you are suffering, that is God's will for you. Hindus, by contrast, will tell you that your suffering is not so much God's fault as yours. They believe in the principle of *karma*—the idea that good or bad actions in a past life affect you in the present. If you are suffering, it is due to the wrong things you have done in the past; it is your fault. Buddhists teach that suffering is some kind of illusion.

illusion. They seem to believe that suffering *appears* to be there, due to our attachment to this world. If you are suffering, it is because you are not meditating enough to be able to transcend this world.

Set in this context, the Bible provides a very good explanation of suffering—although we still have to recognize that, while adequate, it is not complete.

The Bible is explicit that suffering is not God's original will for us. He didn't intend suffering. Rather, he created a perfect world for us. When he created it he said it was good (Gen 1:31). And in this good world, he gave us all things to enjoy (1 Tim 6:17). Nowhere does the Bible say that our suffering is normally God's judgment on us individually because of the things we do. Jesus made that clear when he was asked if the people upon whom a tower had fallen were worse sinners than anyone else (Lk 13:4-5). And nowhere does the Bible teach that our suffering is just an illusion. In fact, the Bible talks a lot about suffering and treats it very seriously.

It is sometimes important to work through this with people so that they are quite sure about what we *don't* believe. Quite often, people seem to think I believe something I don't. They may assume that, because I am a Christian, I must believe that suffering is the judgment of God on us, or that God deliberately causes our suffering in order to teach us and train us. I can appreciate where they have gotten these ideas from, but they need to know that I don't believe them and that I am not asking them to believe them.

A Mucked-Up World

I believe that what the Bible says is this: Suffering has come into the world because the world and everything in it have become mucked up. We live in a world which has, collectively, turned its back on God. Consequently, the world is now full of suffering, pain and death. This is not God's intention, nor is it his capricious judgment on us. Rather, it is the inevitable consequence of our rejection of God. If I decide not to follow the manufacturer's instructions, and fill my car with water instead of gas, I should not be surprised when it won't function properly. This consequence isn't what the manufacturer wanted, nor is it his judgment on me. It is simply what happens when I decide to reject the car's creator.

God didn't create evil, but he did create us with free will. He thus created within us the capacity to create evil by rejecting him. Here lies one of the many mysteries in this area. Why did he give us free will if he knew what we would do with it? There is no complete answer to that. We can see that if God had not given us free will we should not be the real people that we are—with the capacity to think, to decide and, particularly, to love. We can also see that when he gave us free will, God knew that he would have to come in the person of Jesus to die for us in order to rescue us from the mess we would get ourselves into. So he did not give us free will lightly. But these observations don't fully answer the question.

Because we have free will, we are free not only to love but also to do the opposite. We are free to reject God and one another. That is what we have done historically in Adam and Eve, but also personally as we have each continued that rejection. We have tended to use our free will to cause suffering in the world. In fact, the Bible talks about three (partial) explanations for the development of this suffering: through the world, the flesh and the devil. Lets look at those in reverse order (because it's easier that way).

The Bible talks about a real devil, and so did Jesus. I therefore believe that there is a real devil. Some people find that very hard to take. Often, students can just about cope with the fact that I believe in God, but when they find out that I also believe there is a real devil they begin to think I must be certifiably insane. But if you have seen some of the suffering I have seen, you too will probably sometimes find it easier to believe in a devil than in a loving God.

The Bible describes the devil as a roaring lion looking for someone to devour (1 Pet 5:8). He doesn't just want to make life a bit difficult for us. He wants to destroy us. I believe that some suffering is caused by the devil and his evil action in the world.

That raises the question, "Why doesn't God destroy the devil?" As we shall see later, there will come a time when he will do that. But why doesn't he do it now? I wish I could give you a firm answer, but I can't. Could it be that, in some way, the devil is so intricately tied up with this world that to destroy him would also seriously affect us? Or could it be that, in some way, we actually need the devil in order to have real freedom of choice? I find the second possibility much less convincing than the first. But, however we might speculate, we have to admit that this is a mystery, an incompleteness in the explanation.

Of course, we can't blame all suffering on the devil. The cause of suffering is not just out there; it is also within us, in our flesh. The Bible talks about the fact that we cause suffering by the things we do. We were created for love, but our nature has become twisted. We still love, but we have a tendency to love ourselves. Consequently, we often think, say and do things that cause suffering to other people. We may not all get drunk and run over little children, but we do all act in ways which make others suffer, whether by saying unkind things, by overeating while others starve, or by a hundred and one other everyday actions.

Where Was God When ...
Again, why doesn't God stop this suffering? Here there is a more obvious answer, but it still leaves questions. Take a drunk driver who is just about to run over a little child. Couldn't God step in and stop the driver? Of course he could. God can do anything. But suppose he did. What kind of world would we be living in? If God stopped the driver at that point, he would be taking away the driver's free will. For that moment the driver would be like a robot, controlled by God. Now ask yourself what it would be like if God were to step in and stop you anytime you were going to do anything that would cause any suffering to anyone else. How many times would God have had to stop you today? I don't know about you, but I think I would still be lying in bed. I wouldn't have moved. As we shall see later, there will come a time when God will say that enough is enough and he will step in and stop this world. But right now he is delaying that time.

But that doesn't explain why God doesn't step in selectively—not all the time, but just sometimes. And, of course, sometimes he does. There are occasions when God seems to step in miraculously. Why some occasions and not others? I can partially answer this difficult question in terms of God intervening in response to the prayers of his people, but that raises even more questions, and I have to accept that I am still left with mysteries.

Now we come to the third explanation for suffering. We can't explain everything by the action of the devil or our flesh. What about hurricanes, earthquakes and volcanoes? What about cancer, heart disease and babies born blind? Actually, some of these are partially due directly to what we do (if you smoke cigarettes you are more likely to get cancer; if you live in certain areas of the world you are more likely to be killed by an earthquake), but I believe that all of them are indirectly due to the fact that we have all turned our backs on God.

Genesis 3 describes the consequences of our rejection of God. One of these concerns the world itself. "Cursed is the ground because of you," says God (v. 17). It seems that the world itself has become mucked up. This is echoed in the New Testament, which says that the creation itself was "subjected to frustration" (Rom 8:20). When people ask how a God of love could create a world like this, then, we can tell them that he didn't. This world is not how God originally intended it to be, but has become mucked up by our sin.

Of all three explanations, this raises the most difficult questions for me. Although I accept it as a general truth, what am I to believe at a more detailed level? Was there a time when hurricanes and volcanoes did not exist on the earth, or did they always exist but we were originally somehow protected from them? Was there a time when harmful bacteria and viruses didn't exist, or did they always exist but we were originally immune to them? And how can I relate this to modern scientific discoveries about the early earth? I can try to answer these questions by considering the expulsion of Adam and Eve from the protection of the garden as symbolic of God's withdrawing his protection from us in a world that has always been hostile. But I am still left with mysteries.

We have, then, a collection of both mysteries and certainties. I am certain that the explanation the Bible provides is the best and most adequate one going, but it does still leave me with big mysteries. I cannot have a complete explanation of why the loving God allows suffering. But I have to face the fact that suffering exists. I suffer; you suffer; it is a fact of life. The important question is, What is to be done about it? What is the solution to all our suffering?

A Complete Solution

If suffering came into this world because of our rejection of God, there is no reason why we should expect him to sort it out. But, thank God, he is so loving to us that he does provide us with a solution—and a complete one at that.

In fact, God provides two solutions: an "ultimate" one and a "meanwhile" one. This pairing of the ultimate and the meanwhile—the "not yet" and the "now"—is a constant theme throughout God's provisions for us. There are things we have now and things we wait for in faith. We can see this clearly in relation to suffering.

God provides an ultimate solution to suffering. He tells us what will happen at the end of time. As with all good stories, if you want to find what happens at the end, read the end of the book. The book of Revelation tells us that there will come a time when God will destroy this world of suffering, pain and death (21:1). Then he will create a new and perfect world where there will be no more mourning or crying or pain, and we shall live in a proper relationship with God and with one another. At that time he will destroy the devil and all his works, along with this old mucked-up world. That sounds great for everyone. But he will also destroy our mucked-up flesh. That's wonderful for those of us who are Christians, who have received God's forgiveness and look forward to being changed into our new bodies. As Revelation also says, however, only those who have received the new life which Jesus offers will be able to enter this new heaven and earth (21:27). Sin cannot enter it, otherwise it too would be mucked-up immediately.[1]

When we understand that, we realize why God is delaying the time when he will destroy this world—why this ultimate solution is not an immediate one. As Peter says, God is patient with us, giving us time to respond (2 Pet 3:9). In his love, God doesn't want anyone to perish; instead, he wants everyone to come to know him and enter into eternal life with him.

We can go on to see that no matter how much we are suffering here on this earth, we shall not suffer forever. If we receive the new life which Jesus offers, there will come a time when we will be completely set free from our suffering.

Now—and Then

That is great news, particularly for those who struggle in this life. For instance, Jess, a friend of mine who occasionally works with me on my team, was paralyzed in a car accident when she was eighteen. Unless God intervenes with a miracle, Jess (who was studying performing arts) will never walk or dance again on this earth. But she knows that this will not be the case forever. There will come a time when she will get her perfect new body and will dance along with the angels in heaven.

This ultimate solution that we pray for also gives us confidence in our prayers for Christians who are suffering. I often pray for people who are sick, asking that God will heal them. If they are Christians I tell them I am absolutely certain that God will answer this prayer. I have no doubt whatsoever that they are going to be totally and utterly healed. The only question is when. We know they will be totally healed when they get to heaven. All we are asking in prayer is for God to bring that forward to now. It's really a prayer about timing. Sometimes he does, but other times he doesn't. Either way, we know that he will answer this prayer. And, in any case, we are not abandoned in our suffering because, while we wait for the ultimate solution to it, God gives us a "meanwhile" solution.

As we wait for God's ultimate solution to this world, we know that he has not totally abandoned it. There is a sense in which he is still redeeming and transforming this mucked-up old world. In the same way, as we wait for God's ultimate solution to our suffering, we know that he has not abandoned us to it. He is redeeming and transforming our mucked-up bodies. God is currently in the transformation business. Often, he doesn't take away our suffering, but rather transforms it. He takes bad things and turns them into good things.

Let me give you an example from my own life.

Some years ago, Carol and I were eager to have another child. We already had a little boy, Luke, and wanted him to have a brother or sister. No matter what we did, for a long time we just couldn't seem to get pregnant. Eventually, however, Carol did find that she was expecting. We were excited, and so was Luke.

A little while later, Carol started experiencing some pain. Then she started bleeding. After a few hours she miscarried. Out came a tiny baby. Because we were under the care of the consultant at the infertility clinic, I picked up the little baby and wrapped it in kitchen foil. I can't tell you how that broke my heart. I cried and cried over that baby. So did Carol. So did Luke, who sat on our bed, sobbing, "Why did our baby have to die?" That was a good question, and there was no good answer. This death was a bad thing; it was not how God intended it to be.

Through the tears, however, God took this bad thing and transformed it into a good thing. I suddenly realized that our baby had gone straight to heaven. This baby would never experience pain or tears. This baby would never know what it is to be laughed at or rejected. All this baby would know would be good things in the presence of God.

Of course, realizing this didn't take away the pain, but it did transform it. And not just for me. I counsel many young women who have had abortions. I believe they have done a bad thing. Many of them don't need me to tell them that, because they already know it and experience post-abortion trauma. I can, however, tell such a mother my story, and I can encourage her to see that God has taken her bad thing and turned it into a good thing. I believe her baby, like ours, is safe in the arms of Jesus. I encourage her to pray the same prayer Carol prayed night after night as she sobbed, "Lord, please look after my baby."

Jess, too, has seen this transformation in her life. I have known students who were previously hostile to the gospel, but who came to an event just because they wanted to hear what Jess had to say. I can think of one in particular who came back night after night— and in the end became a Christian. This doesn't make Jess's pain any less. She still prays for God to heal her, and she still looks forward to the time when he will. Meanwhile, however, she is experiencing God's transformation of her suffering, as he takes a bad thing and turns it into a good thing.

Perhaps the plainest example of this is death. Death is seen as the ultimate suffering. Yet, for the Christian, death is the ultimate transformation. A few years ago my dad died. When he came out of the hospital for the last time, he told us he didn't want us to pray for him to be healed any more. Instead, he wanted us to pray that he would go comfortably to be with the Lord. Then he said something profound. He told us to cry for ourselves, because we were going to miss him, but not to cry for him, because he couldn't wait to go. He was looking forward to heaven. Death for Dad was not the end but a great new beginning.

No doubt you can think of examples in your own life where God has transformed your suffering. But when you tell people about them, do make sure that you are honest about the pain you felt (and may still feel). And don't be glib about the suffering being experienced by people you are trying to help. You know that, if they became Christians, God could transform their suffering. But they won't be able to see that, and it is not helpful to suggest slick ways in which that might happen.

A seventeen-year-old college student once broke down in tears and told me how her life had fallen apart since she was raped by the leader of a youth camp she had attended when she was fourteen. I gently tried to help her to see that, although nothing could take that experience away, God could transform the suffering into something good, if she would come into a relationship with him. She looked at me with despair in her eyes and asked, "How could anything good ever come out of this?"

I was tempted to answer her question by suggesting possible ways. But that wouldn't have been right. I could listen, but only God could answer that for her. Two days later she became a Christian, and God began that transformation process.

13

Isn't the Bible Full of Errors?

"DON'T QUOTE THE BIBLE TO ME! It's full of contradictions . . . has been changed over the centuries . . . was made up by people who want others to believe it . . . is open to completely different interpretations . . ."* If you have ever spent any time talking about Jesus with people who are thinking seriously about him, you have come across these objections and more.

I am convinced that God has revealed himself to us in Jesus and in the Bible. I am confident that the Bible is reliable and trustworthy in all that it says. But this confidence is not a blind leap of faith or a presupposition with which I have started. Rather, it is a conclusion at which I have arrived. I haven't just accepted the Bible by faith. If I had, I think I would probably have abandoned that faith many times. But the evidence drives me to the conclusion that the Bible is reliable. Of course, I still have many questions about it, and I still struggle with some unresolved problems. Whichever way I look at the evidence, though, I always come back to the conclusion that the Bible is God's reliable and trustworthy communication to us.

If that is a correct conclusion from evidence, and not a presupposition or a blind leap of faith, I must help others to come to that conclusion as well. It is no good just telling non-Christians to accept the Bible (which they won't anyway), or pressing them to believe it as a blind leap of faith (which is not a reasonable request to make of anyone). I must be able to help them think it out and reach that conclusion for themselves.

Some people, I find, have specific questions or objections about particular parts of the Bible, and I must help them with those problems. Most, however, know very little about the Bible and so have more general questions or objections. I try to focus such people on the Gospels as much as possible. This makes the conversation rather more manageable, because we are not jumping all over the place. It also enables us to deal with the most central issue: Jesus. If the Gospel records of Jesus were unreliable, this would cast a major doubt over the whole Bible, since it points to Jesus and leads on from him.

Five Common Questions
People ask me many different questions about the Bible. As in the last chapter, I don't intend to give you pat answers to them. But I hope I can help you with what I have found to be the five most common questions or objections in this area. There isn't enough space in this book to go into each of these questions in detail, but I hope I can at least get you started on each one. At the end of the chapter is a list of books which will give you more complete information.

Reliable Accounts?
1. Were the Gospels written down reliably? Are they accurate records of what really happened? Can we be confident that the Gospels are reliable history? This has got to be the most fundamental question. If we find that the answer is no, it's not really worth looking at the other questions. We might as well give it all up. So I

shall take more space over this than over the other questions. Let's think about four subquestions: (a) When were the Gospels written down? (b) What happened to the stories before they were written down? (c) Could they have been made up or modified by the early church? (d) Is there any external evidence that they were written down reliably?

(a) When were the Gospels written down?

Most people I meet seem to hold the view that the Gospels are unreliable because they were written down a long time after the events they describe. As with many popular views about Jesus, however, the evidence does not support it.

We don't know exactly when the Gospel accounts were written down, because they don't come with a date on them. But we can work out when they are most likely to have been written. We can't come to definite conclusions (as is the case with most historical questions), but we can reach fairly confident ones. We can conclude that the Gospels were probably written down within the thirty-five years following Jesus' death, rather than later than that.

We can attempt to put dates on the Gospels in several different ways. Let me give you two of them.

John Robinson[1] observed that not one New Testament book mentions the destruction of the Jerusalem temple as a past fact. It was a momentous event with massive repercussions for the Jews. Surely, Robinson argues, if it had occurred before the books and letters of the New Testament were written, they would make some reference to it—particularly in Hebrews, which talks such a lot about temple practices. Since we know that the destruction of the temple occurred in A.D. 70, he concludes, the whole New Testament must have already been written by then. In fact, he dates the Gospels even earlier than this.

For an example of another means of dating the Gospels, let's take Luke in particular.

Luke wrote two books which are now contained in the New Testament: his Gospel and the book of Acts. Both were written initially for someone called Theophilus. Luke obviously wrote his Gospel before he wrote Acts, because he begins Acts with the words, "In my former book, Theophilus, I wrote about all that Jesus began to do and to teach." If we can date Acts, then, we can get the latest date by which Luke's Gospel must have been written.

We can attempt to date Acts. The principal character in this book is Paul, whom we follow from just before his conversion, through his three missionary journeys, to Rome, where, we are told, he stayed for two years, preaching the gospel. There the story stops, quite abruptly. Why was this? Why doesn't Luke then tell us of the terrible persecution of Christians in Rome (recorded by the Roman historian Tacitus)? Why doesn't he tell us of Paul's death?

The most likely explanation is that Acts was written before these events took place. When was that? The fourth-century Christian writer Eusebius tells us that Paul died under Nero: "After defending himself the apostle was sent again on his ministry of preaching, and coming a second time to the same city, suffered martyrdom under Nero."[2] Independent histories tell us that Nero died in A.D. 68, so we could conclude that Acts was written before that date. Since Luke was written before Acts, it must have been written some time before A.D. 68.

Having said all this, we do need to recognize that in both these attempts at dating we are using an argument from silence. The first argues from the absence of references to the destruction of the temple, while the second argues from the absence of references to the persecution of Christians and the death of Paul. These are valid approaches to history which are regularly used, though with caution, by historians and archaeologists. But we must realize that we have not firmly established a date for the Gospels. We have simply shown that, given the available evidence, it is most likely that they were written down before the mid- to late 60s A.D. If scholars want to date them later than that (and there was a time when many scholars did), they will have a difficult job explaining why the New Testament does not look back on these events.

(b) What happened to the stories before they were written down?

But what about the period before they were written down? This is usually called the "oral period," the time when the stories were passed on orally. Couldn't they have been made up or changed in that time? This is a possibility we have to explore.

A few years ago, my son particularly enjoyed playing Gossip. Any unfortunate visitor to our house was asked to join us as we sat in a circle and passed around a message by whispering it into the next person's ear. Invariably the end result was pretty garbled. The message had been changed as it was passed on.

This happens not just in party games but also in real life. There's an old story from World War I, when they used to pass messages along the trenches. One such was changed from "Send reinforcements, we're going to advance" to "Send three or four pints, we're going to a dance"! Could something similar have happened to the stories of Jesus before they were written down? Were they corrupted, embellished or otherwise changed in this oral period?

There is no way we could ever know that for sure, but we can consider how likely it would be.

Doing the Numbers

First, we need to ask how long this oral period was. As we have already seen, we can't put a definite time on it. But if the conclusions we drew in the previous section are correct and we are right in dating the Gospels before the mid- to late 60s, and if scholars are correct in dating Jesus' death in A.D. 33, then the oral period would have been no more than thirty-five years.

Second, we need to think whether it is possible for the stories of Jesus to have been transmitted reliably, without being written down, for up to thirty-five years.

We face a problem in attempting to answer this question.

Today, we are surrounded by written and printed information. So we don't need to be good at remembering stories or events. We can always look them up. That's why many people would reply, "No way, I can't even remember information over three years, let alone thirty-five—so how could they?"

But there are things we never seem to forget, and which we pass reliably around the culture without needing to write them down: nursery rhymes, for instance, or playground songs that we learned from someone else, remembered, and then passed on reliably to others. So we *can* do it. If we lived in a culture more like that of Jesus' time, with no printed and very little written information, we would probably be very good at it.

There are some cultures today which have no written material, and I understand they convey stories reliably over long periods of time, as they are carefully and exactly repeated and passed on. I am told that anthropologists who visit a culture and record stories they hear discover, if they revisit the culture many years later, that the same stories are still being recounted in exactly the same way.

Once again, then, although we cannot be certain that the stories of Jesus were not changed before they were written down, there is no reason to assume that they must have been. It is more likely that the early church held the stories of Jesus in such high regard that they made sure they were passed on reliably until they were written down.

(c) Could they have been made up or modified by the early church?

Someone might feel that maybe the early church didn't hold the stories in high regard, or that the church actually edited them or even made them up to bolster its case. Again, this is a popular view. But it does not sit well with the evidence.

Some people reject the Bible out of hand because it was written by people who believed in Jesus. They assume it must be biased and unreliable. When people (quite often) express that view, I generally try to help them think about other literature written by people who believe what they are writing, and I ask them to consider whether they want to reject that also, for the same reason. If we did so, I think we'd have to throw out most of the nonfiction books in every library.

Almost all scientific knowledge, for instance, is based upon the work of scientists who have conducted experiments, come to a conclusion and written it up in a scientific paper. They believe what they are writing. So should we reject them? Can we believe only scientific papers written by people who did not believe their own conclusions? I realize that in some cases we can test the conclusions ourselves by replicating the experiment. But in most cases we just don't have suitable equipment available to us. I don't know about you, but I don't have a particle accelerator in my bedroom. So we have to make a judgment about the trustworthiness of the author.

Are the Authors Reliable?

The important question is not whether the authors believe what they have written down, but how reliable they seem to be as authors. So let's ask that question about Matthew, Mark, Luke and John.

Once again, we cannot be certain that they did not make up or modify the stories of Jesus. But the more I look at the evidence, the more I find that it points to their trustworthiness as authors. For one thing, they often wrote things that worked against them rather than for them. Let me give you three examples.

First, look at the resurrection witnesses. The first people who saw that Jesus had risen from the dead were women. Why is that significant? Because at that time a woman's testimony counted for only half as much as a man's. If the Gospel writers were making this story up, would they have put women as the first witnesses? I don't think so. It weakens their case. Surely the only reason for recording that women were the first witnesses is that this is what actually happened. They were committed to recording it accurately, even if it made their story less readily believable to their contemporaries.

Second, take the fact that Mark records how Jesus called Peter "Satan" (Mk 8:33). There is good evidence that Mark got his information directly from Peter, but even if he didn't, we still have the fact that this writer recorded how Jesus said this terrible thing to Peter. Is this the kind of thing the early church (and particularly Peter himself) is likely to have made up? Again, I don't think so. Doesn't the fact that this was written down for us all to read illustrate their faithfulness in recounting the events, whatever light it shows them in?

Third, consider the fact that they don't take the opportunity to fabricate sayings of Jesus to help them out in times of controversy. Very early in the life of the church the disciples faced a big problem. In fact, they had to call a special council in Jerusalem to sort it out (see Acts 15). The issue was whether new Christians should be circumcised. Now, if the Gospels were really made up or modified by the early church to suit their own ends, wouldn't we expect the writers to have solved this problem by putting something into the mouth of Jesus about circumcision? Jesus never once talked about the importance or otherwise of circumcision (which was a problem for the early church), but he did talk a lot about the Sabbath (which wasn't).[3] Doesn't this suggest, again, that they recorded the events reliably, regardless of how much or how little this helped them?

The evidence, then, does not support the idea that the Gospels were made up or modified by the early church. They contain information that weakens the case of the early church or shows its leaders in a bad light. The writers didn't take the opportunity to put into Jesus' mouth words that would have helped to solve their disputes. All of this points to the Gospel writers as reliable historians.

But that's not the only way of interpreting the data. I talked it through with a group of students in a particularly lively debate some years ago, and they came up with a clever alternative. "Couldn't it be a double bluff?" they suggested. "Perhaps the disciples did make up the whole thing. But they were clever. They knew that if they put these elements in, people would be tricked into thinking that their writing was genuine."

There isn't really an answer to that, except to consider that if that were the case, the disciples must have been not just deceivers but clever, manipulative, scheming deceivers. And then we have to ask what they got out of their deception. Many of the early Christians died terrible deaths because of their beliefs. Of course, this proves nothing if they were themselves unknowingly deceived. But what about the disciples, if they knew they were dying for a lie which they had deliberately set up? Would they have been prepared to hold out for it? We can't prove that they would not have died for such a fabrication, but I would suggest it is very unlikely.

Lies, of course, have a habit of coming out. As Chuck Colson said of his attempt to keep up the lie concerning President Nixon's involvement in Watergate, "We couldn't hold our stories together for three weeks under that pressure. I was around the most powerful men in the world, but we couldn't hold the lie." If the resurrection wasn't true, those disciples could never have held out. Someone would have dug out the tape or something.

(d) Is there any external evidence that they were written down reliably?

The evidence so far supports the conclusion that the Gospels were written down as reliable records of the events which took place. But all this evidence has involved steps of reasoning where we have had to make judgments about the likelihood of competing explanations.

You might now be wondering if there is any other way of testing the reliability of the records. The answer is yes. There are some references in them that we can test archaeologically. Unfortunately, we can't do that for all that the Gospels contain; it simply wouldn't be possible. We can't wind the clock back and see Jesus walking on the water or feeding the five thousand. But there are some elements that we can test by archaeology—places, names, dates.

When we do so, we find that the Gospels are reliable in these areas. And if they are reliable on the points we can test archaeologically, this gives us confidence that they are also likely to be reliable on the points we cannot test in that way. Let me give you two examples.

The first concerns the existence of Pontius Pilate. Until recently, some scholars doubted his existence because of the lack of references to him in Roman records.[4] Could it be that the Gospel writers had made this character up? And if they did, what else had they concocted? In 1961, however, during an excavation in Caesarea, archaeologists discovered a stone which had at one time been built into a building. It still carried part of a carved inscription telling how that building had been dedicated by a certain "Pontius Pilatus, Prefect of Judea."

The second example relates to the pool of Bethesda, where Jesus healed an invalid. The fifth chapter of John's Gospel tells us that this pool was near the Sheep Gate and was surrounded by five covered colonnades, and that sick people needed help to get into the water. Archaeologists have since discovered a double pool with four porticoes around the two sections, and a fifth on the gangway between them. They also found that the pools were some sixteen meters deep—so any invalid would need help not just to get in but also to be supported while in the water.

These are just two examples of many ways in which archaeological discoveries have confirmed dates, names or places in both the Old and New Testaments.

This doesn't mean, however, that there are no unresolved problems in the Bible. There are. For instance, Luke 2 tells us that the census carried out at the time of Jesus' birth was the first one to take place while Quirinius was governor of Syria. There are records of a census that Quirinius carried out in A.D. 6, but this doesn't seem to square with the dates for Jesus, who was born around 6 B.C. It is possible that Quirinius carried out more than one census, and that the one Luke records was (as he says) the first one, followed by a later one in A.D. 6. As yet, we don't know. Until we discover evidence for more than one census, we have to hold this as an unresolved problem.

Even allowing for these uncertainties, the fact remains that the evidence clearly supports the view that the Gospels were written down as reliable records of the events which took place.

Reliable Transmission?

2. Were the Gospels transmitted reliably over the centuries? Do we have now what was written down then, or has it been altered over time? Even if they were written down reliably, are the documents we have now the same as what was written down then?

People often tell me that we can't trust the Bible because so much has been changed as it has been copied, translated, recopied and retranslated. Many seem to assume that the copying and translation have been a serial process, with one copy being copied and translated into another which is then copied and translated into another—and so on. Therefore, they say, as in the game of Gossip, we must now be a long way away from the original. That, however, is not how the process works. Modern copies and translations of the Bible are not taken from recent copies and translations. Rather, scholars work from the earliest available manuscripts in the original languages. And, in recent years, an increasing number of early manuscripts have come to light.

Of course, the only way we could know for certain that we have today exactly what the Gospel writers wrote down so long ago would be if we could discover the very first documents. So far these have not been discovered, and they probably never will be. But we do have manuscript copies which were written down very soon after the original date. Codex Sinaiticus, for instance (kept in the British Museum in London), was written around A.D. 350. The Bodmer papyri and the Chester Beatty papyri were written even earlier—around A.D. 200. The very earliest attested document is the John Rylands fragment, which contains just a few verses of John's Gospel; it was written around A.D. 150.

Given the fact that we are working from these and the thousands of other manuscripts, translations and quotations in early lectionaries, we can be confident that we do have now what was originally written down then. It has not changed over the centuries.

Once again, however, there are some uncertainties. There are, in fact, thousands of variants between the manuscripts. Most of these are differences of spelling or different ways of saying the same thing. Some of them are obvious scribal errors where, in some groups of manuscripts, words have been missed out or misread. These differences and errors are taken into account in modern editions of the Bible, and those of any significance are noted at the bottom of the page. On many pages you will find a footnote beginning "Some manuscripts. . . ." This tells you about a major variant. None of them are of any great importance, except perhaps for the last twelve verses of Mark's Gospel. The earliest and most reliable manuscripts and other ancient sources don't have this ending, and it seems quite likely that it was added subsequently. If you are heavily into handling snakes and drinking poison, the realization that this passage may not be authentic might cause some theological problems for you. But it doesn't worry me.

The existence of these variants does suggest that the early church did not conspire to present a case that justified its own position.

Compare this situation with the actions of Caliph Uthman, who, after the death of Muhammad, decided that only one standard Qur'an must be available, written in Muhammad's own dialect, Quaraish. This was prepared from the version held by Hafsah, one of Muhammad's widows. Then all other versions were burned.

A Bunch of Contradictions

3.What about all the contradictions? Muslims will soon tell you that the Bible cannot be reliable because it now contains contradictions (which, they say, is not the case with the Qur'an). In fact, almost anyone will argue that you can't trust the Bible because it constantly contradicts itself.

In the early days of my ministry, I used to ask people which contradiction they were thinking about. I wasn't trying to trip them up. It was just that I wanted to make sure that I talked about the particular contradiction that interested them. I almost always got the same answer: "Oh, I'm not sure. I can't think of any at the moment, but I know there are loads."

All I managed to do was to make them look stupid. And I then had to give them a few examples of apparent contradictions. So now I usually do that right away, without asking them to name one. Let me do the same for you here.

Mark 5 recounts that when Jesus went across the lake, he met a demoniac, whom he delivered. But when Matthew 8 records what appears to be the same story, it says there were two demoniacs. Isn't that a contradiction? How many demoniacs were there, one or two?

The answer is that we don't know how many demoniacs there were. Probably lots of them lived in that region. Mark tells us of only one, but Matthew speaks of two. For all we know, Jesus could have healed a dozen of them. The accounts are different, but they are not contradictory. They are complementary.

Isn't that the way it works when different people write history? Last week I was speaking at a mission in a medical school. In one of the open debates only two students asked questions, although more were present. Suppose several people each wrote an account of what had happened. One might focus on one of the students and record that "Nick discussed the claims of Jesus with one particular student." Another might focus on both the students and say that "Nick discussed the claims of Jesus with two students." Someone else might refer to the whole group and say, "Nick was talking to a bunch of students." Each of these is a reliable history; they just highlight different aspects of the event. Again, then, we see evidence that the Gospels are reliable history: They have not been carefully edited to make them all say the same thing. They are as one expects to find history written.[5] The Gospels sometimes contain accounts that are complementary but not contradictory.

Other Writings

4. What about the other books, which are not in the New Testament? Don't we have just those books that the early church wanted us to have, and not the others, which tell a different story?

Some say that there *are* contradictory accounts: stories of Jesus that showed a different kind of person, with a different message— the "Gnostic gospels," for instance. Objectors allege that these were not accepted by the church but were repressed. This kind of "conspiracy theory" always makes good journalism, and so it pops up every now and then in the popular press.

It is true that there are other books which claim to be contemporary accounts of Jesus. They are printed in Cartlidge and Dungan's *Documents for the Study of the Gospels,* listed in the "Further Reading" section at the end of this chapter. How do these writings fit in?

First, it shouldn't surprise us that other genuine accounts may be discovered. Luke himself tells us that many had undertaken to write accounts of Jesus before he did (Lk 1:1). Where are they now? Theologians have for years postulated the existence of an earlier Gospel (which they call *Quelle,* a German word meaning "source"—Q for short) from which Matthew and Luke were supposed to have drawn the material common to their Gospels.

We have to ask ourselves, however, whether the Gnostic gospels available today could possibly be genuine. Three questions arise.

First, were they written at the same time as the four Gospels? The answer is that we don't know. It is hard enough trying to date the four New Testament Gospels, let alone the Gnostic ones. But none of them seems to be any earlier than the second century.

Second, were they accepted by the early church? The answer seems to be no. Of course, that could be because the church wanted to suppress them even though they were genuine. But if that were the case, why did they not also suppress those parts of their own Gospels that were (as we have already seen) embarrassing to them? I think it is much more likely that these Gnostic gospels were the products of people who themselves were trying to twist the message of Jesus. Indeed, many of the letters of the New Testament seem to have been written to counter elements that later developed into full-blown Gnostic heresies.

Third, are the contents of the Gnostic gospels consistent with the four Gospels? The answer to this one appears to be yes and no. Some parts seem consistent, but others do not. Take the two gospels of Thomas as an example. The Coptic *Gospel of Thomas,* found in excavations at Nag Hammadi in 1945, is a collection of sayings attributed to Jesus, many of which are consistent with the Jesus we meet in the four Gospels. The Infancy Gospel of Thomas, by contrast, tells of a boy Jesus who gets angry with his playmates and curses them so that they wither or die—and when parents intervene, he gets angry with them too and blinds them. This story is not consistent with the Jesus we meet in the four Gospels.

We have a choice, then. We can accept these other gospels and change our minds about Jesus. Or we can accept the view of the early church that these other gospels are heretical, and we can reject them. Put like that, as a showdown between the four Gospels and the Gnostic ones, it is clear that the evidence for the reliability of the four Gospels is much stronger than the evidence for that of the Gnostic ones. And I join the early church in rejecting the Gnostic gospels as heretical.

More Than a History Book

5. Is the Bible really God's Word? Even if it is accurate history, how can we base our lives on a book written two thousand years ago in a completely different culture?

All that we have seen so far supports the historical reliability of the Gospels. But we could subject any history book to the same kind of examination. The fact that the Bible is a reliable record does not in itself make it God's Word to us. Why do we believe that it is?

The whole Bible claims to be God's Word. I am told (although I haven't counted) that the Bible uses the phrase "Thus says the LORD," or something similar, 3,500 times. Paul says that "all Scripture is God-breathed" (2 Tim 3:16). But anyone could write a book and put claims like that in it. So why should we believe the claims of the Bible?

Once again, let's start with the four Gospels. They record the words of Jesus. Jesus claimed to be God become human, the Son of God. If Jesus was God here on earth and his words were reliably recorded for us, we have in the Gospel accounts the words of God. We have already seen that the gospels are reliable history, and they depict Jesus claiming that he was God-become-human and establishing his claim through his actions. So we can have confidence that we have here the words of God.

Now work backward from the Gospels. Jesus treated the Old Testament as the Word of God. He submitted himself to Scripture (Lk 4:1-12); he said explicitly that in the Psalms David spoke by the Holy Spirit (Mk 12:36); and he called the Old Testament law "the word of God" (Mk 7:13).

Then work forward from the Gospels. Jesus predicted that God would speak to the disciples through his Holy Spirit, who would "teach you all things and . . . remind you of everything I have said to you" (Jn 14:26). This teaching was then written down for us as the New Testament.

This still leaves questions about how the canon of New Testament Scripture was decided on. If that is a particular problem for people, I often suggest that they limit themselves initially to the Gospels. When they have come to understand those, they will see that the rest of the New Testament is entirely consistent with them. Contrary to another popular view, the teaching of Jesus is not different from the teaching of Paul (but there isn't space to look into that here).

If you want to delve into this chapter's topics in more depth, I recommend the books listed below.

* * *

Further Reading on the Reliability of the Bible

Barnett, Paul. *Is the New Testament Reliable?* Downers Grove, Ill.: InterVarsity Press, 1993.

Bivin, David, and Roy Blizzard Jr. *Understanding the Difficult Words of Jesus.* Dayton, Ohio: Center for Biblical Analysis, 1983.

Blomberg, Craig. *The Historical Reliability of the Gospels.* Downers Grove, Ill.: InterVarsity Press, 1987.

Bruce, F. F. *The Book and the Parchments.* London: Marshall Pickering, 1991.

Carson, D. A., and John D. Woodbridge. *Hermeneutics, Authority and Canon.* Leicester, England: Inter-Varsity Press/U.K., 1986.

Cartlidge, David R., and David L. Dungan. *Documents for the Study of the Gospels.* London: Collins, 1980.

Drane, John. *The Bible, Fact or Fantasy?* Oxford: Lion, 1989.

———. *Jesus and the Four Gospels: The Real Evidence.* Oxford: Lion, 1984.

France, R. T. *The Evidence for Jesus.* London: Hodder & Stoughton, 1986.

Greenlee, J. Harold. *Scribes, Scrolls and Scriptures.* Grand Rapids, Mich.: Eerdmans, 1985.

Millard, Alan. *Discoveries from the Time of Jesus.* Oxford: Lion, 1990.

Robinson, John A. T. *Redating the New Testament.* London: SCM, 1984.

Wenham, John. *Redating Matthew, Mark and Luke.* Downers Grove, Ill.: InterVarsity Press, 1992.

14

Can You Prove It?

"PROVE IT TO ME. I'LL ONLY BELIEVE if you can prove it." **If** I could have a night at home with Carol for every time I hear that demand when I'm away on a mission, I'd be a happy man.

There's a sense in which I have to admit defeat right away when people demand that I prove Christianity to them. I can't. But then, I can't actually prove anything! And neither can they.

I can't even prove that I exist, let alone anything else. Lao-tse, a great Chinese philosopher, illustrated it this way: "If, when I am asleep, I am a man dreaming that I am a butterfly, how do I know when I am awake that I am not a butterfly dreaming I am a man?" The answer is that you don't. You can't actually prove it. If you were to study philosophy, you would probably spend a lot of time trying to prove your own existence—and finding that you can't.

Of course, that doesn't mean that philosophers believe we don't exist. No, they recognize that the problem lies not in our existence but in the demand for proof. We can't prove that we exist, but there is good evidence that convinces us that we do. If you are not sure of that, let me poke you in the eye with a sharp stick and see if you change your mind.

The fact is that we don't live our lives on the basis of proof, but by taking a step of faith based upon reasonable evidence. We do it all the time. When you sat down, you took a step of faith that the chair would hold you; when you ate your last meal, you took a step of faith that the food was not poisoned. These were reasonable steps of faith: the chair looked strong enough, and the food seemed all right. But the fact is that you couldn't *prove* it before you actually sat down or ate. You simply took a step of faith on the basis of reasonable evidence.

All I am asking people to do is to treat a decision about Jesus in the same way as every other choice about life. The problem is that so many people make an unfair shift. They live the rest of their lives by taking steps of faith based upon reasonable evidence, but when it comes to Jesus they want absolute proof.

Sometimes I try to help people see this inconsistency by asking what it would be like if they demanded proof of everything else. They would end up like the Greek philosopher Cratulus, who swore that he would never say anything unless he could be absolutely sure of the truth—and was reduced to silently wagging his finger. Or they would be like Mark Twain who, when still a journalist, was told by his editor never to report anything as a fact unless it had been verified, and therefore wrote a story which ran as follows:

A woman giving the name of Mrs. James Jones, who is reported to be one of the social leaders of the city, is said to have given what purported to be a party yesterday to a number of alleged ladies. The hostess claims to be the wife of a reputed attorney.

When people ask me for proof, therefore, I try to help them to see that what they really need to look for is not absolute proof but reasonable evidence. It is a bit like being in court. The lawyer can't prove that Joe Bloggs murdered Fred Smith, but he can present evidence to be considered. Perhaps Joe Bloggs hated Fred Smith. Perhaps he had threatened to kill him. Perhaps he was there at the time of the murder. Perhaps he was found with the smoking gun in his hand. Perhaps he turned to the police and said, "It's a fair arrest, officer. I did it." But even then, the lawyer still hasn't proved it in the absolute sense. He has simply shown that the evidence is overwhelming.

It is the same with Jesus. I can't prove to people that the message of Jesus is true. But I think that if we look at the evidence we shall find it overwhelming—so much so that it is not unreasonable to take the step of faith required to entrust ourselves into Jesus' hands. It is then, as we enter into a relationship with Jesus, that we experience the truth of the gospel. We still haven't proved it absolutely, but we have a confident assurance based upon reasonable evidence and personal experience.

Overwhelming Evidence
Let me give you an illustration I often use when I try to help people to grasp this concept.

I have a young daughter called Lizzie. How can I prove to you that Lizzie exists? Suppose I start by pointing you to objective evidence. I might show you her birth certificate, or diaries, or photos. The problem with all this objective evidence is that it could be explained away. You could say that the birth certificate is a fake, the diaries are phony and the photos are of another baby.

Suppose, then, I take a different approach and tell you about my personal experience of Lizzie. I could tell you how she runs to me when I come home and calls out, "Cuggle, Daddy, cuggle!"

But you could explain these away. You might say I was lying or deluded. "Yes, you *think* you have a baby daughter—and I expect you also think you have a six-foot white rabbit called Bernard."

So far, I haven't done very well. Although I have presented good evidence, it hasn't convinced you. But there is one way you could be sure that Lizzie exists. You could come over to my house and meet her. She could sit on your lap (and wet on you!). Then you'd know that she exists; you would have come into a personal relationship with her. You still haven't proved it absolutely. You could be deluded, or you could have experienced some very good virtual reality or a hallucination—or you might not even exist yourself. But you do now have a confident assurance based upon reasonable objective evidence, other people's testimony and your own personal experience.

It seems to me that it is the same with Jesus. I can present the objective evidence for Jesus. I happen to think that this is very strong. In fact, I would say that there is overwhelming objective evidence that Jesus Christ historically walked on this earth, historically died on the cross and historically rose to life. We can know that he is Lord and King, and therefore we must respond to him in repentance and faith.

But for most non-Christians this is not enough. They want more. So I can tell them about my personal experience of Jesus. Again, I would say that this evidence is overwhelming. For years now I have trusted God to provide the money I need to live and carry out my ministry. If it's not there, I don't eat. Yet I haven't starved. But again, for many people this is not enough. And, to be fair, how do they know that I am not lying or deluded? Ultimately, they will be confident of the truth of the gospel only as God opens their eyes and enables them to respond to him.

I know this idea can be very difficult for people to accept. Many have said to me, "I want to know for certain that it's true before I become a Christian. I don't want to become a Christian in the hope of coming to know that it's true." But that isn't possible—with Jesus or with anything else in life. As I mentioned earlier, I am only asking them to do with Jesus what they do in the rest of their lives. They might say, "I want to know for certain that this chair will hold me before I sit on it," but they will actually know that for certain only when they take a step of faith and sit on it. Of course, I am not suggesting that they should blindly sit on any old chair, no matter how rickety it looks. That's not a step of faith; that's a leap in the dark. They must look at the objective evidence to assess how strong it seems to be, and they would do well to listen to other people about what happened when they sat on it. But ultimately there will come a time when they have to sit down for themselves. And there will come a time when they have to trust in Jesus for themselves.

What Evidence Do You Want?

Having said all this, there are times when I take a different approach. Occasionally, if people insist that they want proof, I ask them just what kind of proof they would like.

Some years ago, for instance, a group of students were quite dogmatic that they would believe in God only if he proved himself to them. "OK," I said, "let's set a test for God. What evidence would you need to convince you that God is really there?"

For a minute they looked puzzled. In all their demands for proof, they had never considered what kind of proof they were looking for.

One of them piped up: "I'll believe only if he shows himself—if he turns up here."

"OK," I responded, "let's imagine he does. Suppose someone walks in through that door and says he is God. Will you believe him?"

It didn't take long for them to reply to that suggestion. "Of course not. There are loads of lunatics who think they are God."

"Quite right," I replied. "So what would he have to do to prove that he is God?"

They thought for a moment. Then one of them said, "He'd have to do something miraculous to show his power—turn this Coke into vodka, or something."

Another interrupted him. "No, that's no good, because he could be a trickster or a magician."

How perceptive she was. The ability to impress us doesn't necessarily mean that someone is God. I'm incredibly impressed by the things David Copperfield does, but I don't think he is God. I continued to try to help these students think what kind of evidence they would need to be sure that this person really was God.

Eventually, after a lot of prompting, they hit upon something. "God is immortal," they said. "He cannot die. So what we would need to do is to try to kill him and find that we can't."

"That's a good one, isn't it?" I replied. "But couldn't that just be due to our inability to kill him, not to his immortality? Wouldn't it be a better test if we did kill him, and he was dead for several days, but then he came back to life again?"

"Yes," they said. "Then we would know."

"Right," I replied. "Let's be clear about this. What you are saying is that you will believe in God only if he turns up on the earth, claims to be God, does some miracles, is then killed and a few days later comes back to life again."

Their expressions changed as they saw where they had led themselves.

"Guys," I said, "you are in luck. God has already done it!" God has already given us all the evidence we could ever reasonably require, no matter how skeptical we are.

When I went through this with a group of youngsters aged fourteen to fifteen, from a rough housing project, they were even more demanding than the students with whom I usually work. They wouldn't accept this person's coming back to life as final, convincing evidence. "He could be the man's twin brother pretending to be him," they said.

"OK," I replied. "To stop that, let's lock the dead man's body in a cupboard."

"Ah!" they said. "The twin brother could get him out of the cupboard."

"So let's put guards on the cupboard."

"But the guards could be in on it too."

"OK, let's choose guards from a rival gang, and let's put them under sentence of death if they allow anyone to get to the body. Would you be convinced then?"

"Yes," they said. "That would do it."

And of course they are still in luck, because all those things (except that it was a tomb and not a cupboard) happened to Jesus too.

Evidence Is Not Enough

It's important not to get overexcited here. This approach may sound slick and convincing (and for that reason I only rarely use it). But giving people convincing evidence is not enough. Perhaps it is significant that wherever I have used this approach, I have never once seen anyone so convinced as to ask, "What must I do to be saved?" It is important to answer people's questions and to show them that God has given us plenty of evidence so that we may know that the gospel is true. But this in itself will not make people become Christians. We need God to open their eyes, and we need them to be prepared to change. For there is also a moral dimension.

Back in chapter two we saw that most people choose their worldview in order to enable them to live the way they want. Rarely do people think, *I believe this, so how must I live?* Rather, they seem to think, *This is how I want to live. What do I have to believe in order to justify this behavior?*

The same is true of the way people respond to the evidence for Jesus. I have spent countless hours helping people to look at evidence and reach a reasoned conclusion about Jesus. Rarely have I then heard people say, "I have looked carefully at all the evidence and come to the conclusion that the message of Jesus is not true." Of course they wouldn't, because the evidence is overwhelming. I have, however, often heard people say, "I have looked carefully at the evidence and come to the conclusion that the message of Jesus is indeed true—but I still don't want to become a Christian." And the reason is simply that they don't want to change the way they lead their lives. They reject the truth so that they can carry on living the way they want rather than accept the truth and let Jesus change them.

Of course, this doesn't apply just to non-Christians. I have seen Christians follow the same pattern. I used to know a well-respected minister who had a very strict Reformed theology. I was staggered to hear that he is now a woolly liberal who has rejected his previous firm beliefs. Why was this? What had brought about the change? Was it that he had looked at new evidence and reassessed his beliefs? No. He had begun an adulterous affair with a member of his congregation, and he didn't want to give it up. His long-held beliefs no longer fitted with his behavior. He had a choice: he could change his behavior back to fit his beliefs, or he could change his beliefs to fit his new behavior. He chose the latter.

Jesus said, "If they do not listen to Moses and the Prophets, they will not be convinced even if someone rises from the dead" (Lk 16:31). So, no matter how much convincing evidence we give people, we still need to pray that God will open their eyes and that they will respond.

Sometimes it does happen, and people we have been helping want to become Christians. For me it has happened even in large open debates. Among all the probing questions, a student will suddenly say, "This is all making sense to me. What do I need to do to become a Christian?" What a great question to be asked! And we must be able to give a clear answer. That is what the final part of this book is about.

Part Four

Helping People Who Want to Become Christians

15

Leading
Someone to
Faith in Christ

WHAT CAN WE DO WHEN SOMEONE we are helping wants to become a Christian? How do we take our friend through that process?

Just as there is no one formula for helping people to understand the gospel, there is no one formula for helping people to take that step of faith to become Christians. The Bible does not contain a universal "sinner's prayer" that we have to pray in order to enter God's kingdom. The thief on the cross next to Jesus just said, "Remember me when you come into your kingdom" (Lk 23:42). But Jesus warned us that "not everyone who says to me, 'Lord, Lord,' will enter the kingdom of heaven" (Mt 7:21). It is the response of our hearts that matters, more than the words of our mouths.

As before, I am not going to give you a set of pat statements and prayers to use. Instead, I will try to give you an idea of an approach which I often (but not always) find appropriate.

Do They Really Mean It?

First of all, I want to help people be sure that they are indeed ready to make this step of commitment to Christ. Jesus made it very clear that we must count the cost of following him (see, for instance, Lk 14:25-33). You may think I am a terrible evangelist, but when people tell me they want to become Christians I often begin by trying to put them off. I tell them that if they follow Jesus they will be swimming against the tide for the rest of their lives. The world is going one way, and they are choosing to go another. They may well find that if they become identified with Jesus, the world that rejected him will begin to reject them too.

People must be sure that they know the implications of the step they are taking. I don't want to risk their becoming "stillborn Christians." I meet too many who tell me that they once prayed a prayer of commitment but nothing happened.

If it becomes clear that they are not ready to take that major step, I invite them to take whatever step they can, with integrity. During one mission I sat in a student coffee bar with a young woman who told me that she had been impressed by all she had heard and read about Jesus, and that she wanted to become a Christian. But she knew she wasn't ready to take that step. I struggled, trying to help her. And then it suddenly came to me. I took her to Ephesians 5, where Paul talks about our relationship with Jesus being rather like marriage.

"And that's the problem," she said. "I don't feel ready to get married to Jesus."

"I understand that," I replied, "and I don't want to push you into it. But are you perhaps ready to start going out with Jesus?" Her face brightened. "Yes," she said. "I can do that."

We found a quiet corner, and she prayed to Jesus, saying that when she becomes a Christian she wants to mean it, but for now she wanted to start developing a relationship with him. After she had prayed, I talked with her about what it might mean to "go out" with Jesus—to spend time with him, to talk to him (in prayer) and to listen to him talking to her (primarily through the Bible). The mission came to an end, and I haven't seen any more of her. But I pray that soon she will find herself ready to take that major step of faith to become a Christian.

When They Are Ready

What do we do when people are ready to take that step? How do we help them?

In all the stages we have talked about so far, we have been trying to point them to Jesus and not to ourselves. Now, at this crucial stage in particular, I want to help them to do what the Bible says and not what I say. Although there is no set "sinners' prayer" in the Bible, there is a clear and simple command, which Jesus set out right at the beginning of his ministry. He said, "Repent and believe the good news" (Mk 1:15). The gospel centers around "Jesus Christ and him crucified" (1 Cor 2:2). Our response to discovering that Jesus is the Christ is to repent, and our response to his crucifixion is to receive the forgiveness he has made available for us.

However I lead people to faith, I want to be sure that they finally understand that they are repenting of all their sin and receiving forgiveness, not on the grounds of anything they are doing, but on the grounds of Jesus' death for them on the cross. And I want, if possible, to focus them on information coming from the Bible rather than from me. Here is one way in which I sometimes do so.

If they ask, "What must I do to become a Christian?" I point out that other people asked exactly the same question in the Bible, and the answer they were given is recorded for us there. I then get them to look with me at Acts 2:37, which says, "When the people heard this, they were cut to the heart and said to Peter and the other apostles, 'Brothers, what shall we do?'"

Now, let's see what Peter told them to do. The answer comes in the next verse: "Peter replied, 'Repent and be baptized every one of you, in the name of Jesus Christ for the forgiveness of your sins. And you will receive the gift of the Holy Spirit.'" Before I guide them through this step, I point out the next verse, which says that this offer was not just for those people there in Jerusalem but is for everyone—and that includes them. Verse 38, then, tells us that we are to *do two things* and to *receive two things.* We are to repent and be baptized; we are to receive the forgiveness of our sins and the gift of the Holy Spirit. I then help inquirers to understand each of these four points.

To *repent* means literally to "change your mind." It is about change, and it is our minds that need to be changed. If people are serious about becoming Christians, they will want to change. They will have realized that they are doing things that are wrong, and they will want to start doing what is right. Indeed, if they know anything about relationships, they will know that all relationships mean change. When people start going out with a new girlfriend or boyfriend, they don't stay the same; they change. So when we enter into a relationship with the holy, living God, of course we expect to have to change.

We need to understand what it is that has to change. It is our minds. It is not initially our behavior that has to change. Although, once our minds have changed, our behavior will gradually follow, God does not require us to achieve a certain standard of behavior in order to be acceptable to him. All he asks is that we change our minds, so that we don't want to do what is wrong and we do want to do what is right. Similarly, it is not primarily our emotions that have to change. Although once our minds have changed, our emotions will gradually follow, God does not require us to have certain types of feelings in order to come to know him. All he asks is that we change our minds, so that we want to feel the same way that he does.

When people are sure that they want to change their minds, they can move on to the second thing they have to do, which is to be baptized. Does this mean that they have to run down to the local river in order to become Christians? Not necessarily. Although baptism is important, what matters at this stage is the fact that it was a public sign. Are they prepared to acknowledge publicly that they are following Jesus?

Many people tell me that their faith is personal and private. Well, the Bible says they are half-right. Our faith must be personal—but not private. Baptism in Acts 2 was not a private affair carried out in a little church with the doors closed. It was a public event carried out in an open river. Following this principle, are people ready to identify themselves publicly as Christians, ready to let others know that from now on they want to follow Jesus? If so, we can move on to the two things God has promised us.

First, he promises that we shall receive forgiveness of our sins. Because Jesus died for us, we can be forgiven for everything wrong we have ever done. Usually, when people are at this stage, they already understand what that means. But I am particularly eager to help them see that they are receiving forgiveness because of what Jesus did for them on the cross, not because of a particular prayer which they are praying now. They are receiving what God has made available for them. They cannot earn it, but they do need to ask for it.

Second, he promises that we shall receive the gift of the Holy Spirit. God promises not just to forgive us our sins but also to come and live inside us by his Holy Spirit, so that we are able to change and have the power to live in his world his way. Again, people usually already have a clear understanding of what this means. But I am anxious to help them see what God does *not* promise them. I ask them to look carefully at the verse and to notice that it does not say, "You will receive a warm fuzzy feeling." In fact, it doesn't say anything about feelings at all.

Some people, when they become Christians, experience a strong, even overwhelming, feeling. Others don't. It's just like getting married. As a boy, I sang in the parish church choir, and I must have seen hundreds of weddings. I noticed that some couples, when they got married, clearly experienced a tremendous feeling. Some laughed, some cheered, some even fainted. But most people didn't appear to feel anything special. They can all have been in no doubt, however, that through the vows they had declared and the promises they had received, they were indeed married. In the same way, people have different experiences when they enter into a relationship with God through Jesus. But whatever they feel or don't feel, if they have truly repented and asked God to forgive them, they can be sure that they are now Christians.

Helping Them Take That Step

Once someone understands what he has to do, how can we help him to take that great step of faith? I usually ask outright something like this: "Are you ready to become a Christian? If you are not, I'm not here to push you. But if you are, I am here to help you." If the reply is yes, I suggest a way of proceeding.

I invite the person to pray with me, in his own words, out loud. I stress that the words of the prayer don't really matter, but that he might want to say something about wanting to repent and receive the forgiveness Jesus provides, asking God to forgive him and give him the Holy Spirit. I emphasize, however, that the prayer is not meant to be a memory test. He doesn't have to say all those four things, but he does need to mean them. I then suggest that, to make it easier, I could pray for him before he prays, and again afterward. If he is happy with that, I often put a hand on his shoulder just to show that I am there, identifying with him, and pray something like this: "Lord, thank you for [the person's name]. Thank you that he wants to come to you. You know how nervous he is. Please help him to be able to pray to become a Christian now." I then say something like "Come on, now you pray."

Then the person prays. If you have never been with someone when he or she prays to become a Christian, you have never experienced one of the greatest thrills in evangelism. I have led countless people to faith in Christ over the years, but their prayers never fail to move me. I sometimes even cry—but that helps them, because they sometimes do too!

Once the person has prayed, I pray for him. And I ask God to give me a Bible verse as a particular word for this individual at this time.

What Do I Do Now?
In one sense that is the end of the evangelism story. Your friend has now moved from the kingdom of darkness into the kingdom of light. But in another sense it is just the beginning. As he takes his first steps in his new life with Jesus, he still needs help. He needs to know how he can go on and grow in his new faith.

Over the years, I have led many people in prayers of commitment to Christ. I have often found that, once they have prayed, they look up at me and say, "What do I do now?" Usually we read Acts 2:42, where we see that the new Christians did four things. They devoted themselves to the apostles' teaching, to the fellowship, to the breaking of bread and to prayer. In the same way, all of us, but new Christians especially, need to devote ourselves to those four things. Listed below are some booklets that will help you get your friend started on the path of discipleship.

* * *

Booklets to Use with New Christians

(All are available from InterVarsity Press, P.O. Box 1400, Downers Grove, IL 60515)
Stott, John R. W. *Being a Christian.*
Christ in You.
Griffiths, Michael. *Encouraging New Christians.*
Clark, Kelly James. *Quiet Times for Christian Growth.*

Postscript

Maintaining Motivation

I AM WRITING THIS POSTSCRIPT in yet another room in yet another university. This time I am at St. Andrews, where I am coming to the end of a week-long mission. Through the week, we have seen many people take significant steps toward faith in Jesus, and we have seen a few become Christians. That is marvelous news. But it has also been hard. Here I am, once again, miles away from home, facing the constant struggle of evangelism. Why do I keep doing it? Why do we all keep doing it?

I have often lost my motivation for evangelism, usually because I have had an inadequate motive for it. If we have the right motive, we'll have no problem with motivation.

For a long time, my motive for evangelism was centered upon the results I hoped to achieve. I was not alone in that. Many of us get involved in evangelism because we want to see people become Christians. Now, don't get me wrong. We are right to be delighted when people become Christians. If we want to see people come to faith, we want what God wants. The Bible says that God doesn't want anyone to perish; he wants everyone to come to repentance (2 Pet 3:9).

But if the results we hope to achieve are our prime motive for evangelism, what happens when people don't become Christians? What do we do when we appear to be unsuccessful, when it seems so tough, when we don't see any fruit for our labors? Well, let's be honest. We all know what we do. We give up.

After a while, I developed a new motive for evangelism. It wasn't success, but duty. Jesus commands us to go out and make disciples (Mt 28:19). That is a command. It is not an option. I want to obey Jesus, so I want to get on with evangelism. Whether or not I see people become Christians, I will carry on, because it is my duty. That sounds impressive. But the problem with that motive for evangelism is that we soon become dry and hard. We may keep on with evangelism; we don't give up, but there is no life or vitality in it. We have a form of evangelism, but no power.

So what should be our motive for evangelism? The answer is this: love. In his second letter to the church at Corinth, Paul says that it is Christ's love that compels him (2 Cor 5:14). I pray for that same motive. I still want to see people become Christians, and I still want to obey Jesus. But most of all, I pray for a passionate love for people who are not Christians. Then I shall never want to give up because of a lack of fruit, nor will I carry on out of a dry sense of duty. Instead, I will be highly motivated by love to keep on at it, whatever hardships I face.

I urge you to join me in praying that God will give you such a passionate love for people—that you, like Paul, will find that this love compels you. And if you have found this book helpful, will you pray that prayer for me also? I, too, need your prayers—so that I may find evangelism slightly less difficult.

Notes

Introduction
[1]I am very grateful to Canon John Chapman for teaching me this lesson in the early days of my ministry.

Chapter 2: What Has Gone Wrong?
[1]Everyone has his or her own self-sustaining feedback loop, including us Christians. But that doesn't mean that our Christian worldview is necessarily wrong. It does mean, however, that we need to ask ourselves difficult questions so that we can let go of beliefs that are solely self-sustaining and hold on to only those which are self-sustaining and also true. We shall look at this in some more depth in chapter eight.

Chapter 4: Where Do I Start?
[1]See Francis Crick, *The Astonishing Hypothesis* (New York: Simon & Schuster, 1994); Roger Penrose, *The Emperor's New Mind* (New York: Vintage, 1990); Nicholas Humphrey, *Soul Searching* (North Pomfret, Vt.: Trafalgar/Chatto & Windus, 1995).

Chapter 6: But They Won't Listen!
[1]We may find, as postmodernism develops, that we have to contend for rationality itself. And since our assurance of rationality is rooted in the belief that we are created in the image of God, we may find ourselves in pretty sparse company as we do that.
[2]Hegel was a nineteenth-century German philosopher who is perhaps best known for his view that ideas develop through a process whereby a thesis (a starting idea) generates an antithesis (a contradictory idea), which combines with the thesis to form a synthesis.

Chapter 8: We Can Be Wrong Too
[1]Origen was a third-century theologian and biblical scholar who had himself castrated, mistakenly believing that this was what God required of him.
[2]See John Stott's comments in David L. Edwards and John Stott, *Evangelical Essentials: A Liberal-Evangelical Dialogue* (Downers Grove, Ill.: InterVarsity Press, 1988), especially chapter six.
[3]Nihilism is the name given to a philosophical position which rejects all religious

and moral principles and may even deny that anything has real existence.
[4]Named after Pyrro of Elis, who lived in the third century B.C.
[5]For a consideration of skepticism (from a non-Christian perspective), see Paul Kurtz, *The New Skepticism: Inquiry and Reliable Knowledge* (New York: Buffalo, 1994).
[6]Reductionism, in its strong form, is the principle that complex problems can be solved only by reducing them to lower, simpler levels.

Chapter 9: Do I Understand It?
[1]Once again I am grateful to Canon John Chapman, who first introduced me to this very helpful summary.

Chapter 12: If God Is So Good, Why Is the World So Bad?
[1]You might like to think about whether we shall have free will in heaven and, if so, whether we will just rebel once more and so start the cycle all over again. Or is it the case that we won't have free will? If we won't, how can we be real people, with the capacity to love? That one should keep you awake for a while.

Chapter 13: Isn't the Bible Full of Errors?
[1]See John A. T. Robinson, *Redating the New Testament* (London: SCM, 1976). This is a significant book in that Robinson, as one of the early popularizers of liberal theology, is not stating an argument because he wants to justify a conservative evangelical approach to the Bible, but rather because the facts speak for themselves and point to an early date of writing.
[2]Eusebius, *Ecclesiastical History* 2.22.
[3]In fact he only once mentions circumcision (Jn 7:22-23)—when he is really talking about the Sabbath!
[4]Tacitus, the Roman historian, refers to him, but only in the passage where he is talking about Jesus (or Chrestus, as he calls him); so some have argued that this really came from Christian sources.
[5]Once again, if people argue that this is a clever double-bluff, I would ask them to consider whether the disciples would deliberately scheme and lie like this and then die for the belief they knew to be a lie.